REAL ESTATE CONTRACTS HANDBOOK

(Ninth Edition)

Your Guide to Writing Clear, Concise and Correct Real Estate Contracts – and more

By

Craig E. Buck, Attorney

ABOUT THE AUTHOR: C   an owner of Alliance Title & Escrow and partner in The Buck Law   ecializing in real estate, and real estate closings with offices at:

6800 Backlick Rd. #205 Spri   ia 22150 (703) 451-5203
1109 Heatherstone Dr. Frede   ginia 22407 (540) 785-6575

Craig E. Buck was twice Past Chairman of the Northern Virginia Association of Realtors® Standard Forms Committee and is a lecturer and teacher for real estate and legal continuing education.   He has received the Northern Virginia Association of Realtors® Affiliate of the Year Award.

E-Mail: ReaLawBuck@aol.com

Website: www.VirginiaClosings.com

Published by Brigade Press
130 Caroline St.
Fredericksburg, Virginia 22401

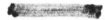

ISBN 9780971069701

Library of Congress Control Number 2011904356

DISCLAIMER

From a Declaration of Principles jointly adopted by a Committee of the American Bar Association and a Committee of Publishers and Associations:

This publication is designed to provide accurate and authoritative information in regard to the subject matter covered. It is sold with the understanding that the publisher is not engaged in rendering legal, accounting or other professional service. If legal advice or other expert assistance is required, the services of a competent professional person should be sought.

Some final cautions -- Laws vary from state to state and the material presented may not be appropriate in all jurisdictions. This material is for EDUCATIONAL PURPOSES ONLY AND THERE IS NO WARRANTY, EXPRESS OR IMPLIED, THAT IT WILL ACCOMPLISH YOUR INTENDED RESULT. This material cannot take the place of professional advice including competent legal counsel. Know your limitations and do not hesitate to discuss your problem with your agent, broker, or attorney.

HOW TO USE THIS MATERIAL

This book is divided into six sections. The first two are cross-referenced to deal with specific fact situations.

Section One, Contract Considerations, explains contracts and the various clauses found in pre-printed forms. This book does not try to create a contract from scratch. There are too many variations in state laws and practices. It is assumed you are working from a form customary to your jurisdiction. We will endeavor to provide those clauses that might not be included in your standard form.

Brackets [   ] refer to numbered clauses in Section Two.

Section Two, divides Suggested Clauses, by subject matter. This section includes many issues that are not part of pre-printed contracts. The major topics are alphabetized. Check the Table of Contents for individual clauses.

Section Three, Articles, includes articles on agency, FHA loan payoffs, rollover of gain on the sale of a personal residence, equity sharing, tax deferred exchanges and many more topics.

Section Four, Agreements contains the sample forms including a Letter of Intent, Joint Ownership Agreement, Note, Deed of Trust, Lease and other forms. You MUST review these forms with a local attorney before using them. They are samples and may not be appropriate for your particular jurisdiction.

Section Five, is the "Ten Secrets" series.

Section Six is the real estate dictionary.

Tables showing 15 and 30 year loan payments are at the back of the book.

REAL ESTATE CONTRACTS HANDBOOK

TABLE OF CONTENTS
References are to page numbers.

SECTION TWO - SUGGESTED CONTRACT CLAUSES

SECTION ONE - CONTRACT CONSIDERATIONS - HOW TO WRITE A CLEAR CONCISE AND CORRECT CONTRACT

A contract is set of legally enforceable promises. For these, the law recognizes a duty and, if there is a breach, will give a remedy.

No particular form is required but, in most jurisdictions, contracts for the sale of real estate must be in writing. Oral agreements and representations are not binding. This is called the Statute of Frauds.

In most cases, courts will only look within the four corners of the document to determine the parties' intent. Evidence outside the four corners is called "parole evidence" and is not admissible except to resolve ambiguities. This exception can overwhelm the rule in some jurisdictions so your best bet is to make sure there are no ambiguities.

Simply put, a good contract is one that accurately and completely expresses the understandings and agreements of the parties. Everything is written down as the parties' intended and there are no ambiguities.

Agreement is the key word and that requires a mutual meeting of the minds. Most contract disputes are not the consequence of cheating or fraud. Disputes develop because there really was not an agreement. There are two ways this can happen. First, ambiguous contract terms can mean different things to different people. Second, the contract may not address important issues or anticipate unexpected changes.

An agent doesn't know what the buyer and seller think or expect. The buyer and seller often never meet. The normal give and take process of offer, counter-offer and acceptance does not necessarily lead to an agreement although it may birth a signed document. What good is a signed document if the parties don't agree on what it means? It is a liability and therefore, worse than worthless because now you have a fight on your hands.

If there is a dispute and the terms are ambiguous, a court will determine the intent of the parties. That is extremely difficult and may lead to all sorts of mischief as the parties decide what they "must have" meant.

This book does not create a contract from scratch. There are too many variations in state laws and practices. It is assumed you are working from a form customary to your jurisdiction. We will endeavor to provide those clauses that might not be included in your standard form.

Working from a standard form affords some protection but there are always those pesky areas that require a handwritten clause. Often, the standard form does not address a particular need. It is here that agents stumble and wise men fear to tread. So, here are some simple tips to keep you out of trouble.

Tip #1 SAY EVERYTHING YOU NEED TO SAY Don't be reluctant to spell contract terms out in detail. For example, contingencies need an IF followed by a THEN and a WHEN. Ink is cheap - until you write a check to cover a mistake.

Tip #2 Try to write contracts that ADDRESS THE ISSUES. Make people commit to the hard choices before they sign. Deal with all possibilities. A good example is the pre or post-occupancy agreement. If you think you will need one, it should be part of the original contract, not an afterthought negotiated later.

Tip # 3 AVOID AMBIGUOUS SUBJECTIVE WORDS such as "satisfactory" or "reasonable." They mean entirely different things to different people.

HOW DO YOU DO IT?

First, you must understand the contract. Read it from beginning to end, paragraph by paragraph. Think about each provision and make sure you know what it says and means. That may seem obvious but most disputes are resolved by answers in the form itself. You're not expected to memorize the contract but it helps to know the answer is "in there somewhere" so you can go look. I can never remember if a termite inspection is good for 30 days or 60 days or whatever, but I know the answer is in the contract form and I have an idea where to look for it.

Second, learn to question. Address all the important issues and anticipate the unexpected. Look into the future and ask, "what if?" Plan for the worst.

Third, be sure everyone understands their respective responsibilities.

The following comments clarify common pre-printed contract clauses and point out areas that may deserve special attention. Many are elementary but easy to forget. Use this section as a checklist. The categories are in the order they appear in many contracts.

Suggested numbered clauses from this book appear in brackets [ ].

NAMES

Purchaser's Name - List all purchasers and borrowers. The buyer may have trouble obtaining a loan unless all necessary parties are willing to execute the loan documents at settlement. If the contract will be assigned to another party, be sure to provide for that in the original offer. An Assignment form is included in the FORMS section of this Handbook.

Seller's Name - Be precise or the title examiner can be hopelessly confused. Joe Smith could be Joseph Smith, and either one could be a Senior or Junior.

Check for any deaths, marriages, divorces or name changes. We had a case where Wife #2 had the same name as former Wife #1 and it was former Wife #1 on title. If #2 had signed our Deed, #1 would still have an interest in the property. Account for all parties and their spouses even if they are not named on the title. In many states, a spouse has an interest in the property even if they are not on the title. If the Sellers have divorced, do not rely on a property settlement agreement alone to eliminate a spouse's interest. A court may have decreed the wife gets the house, but until the husband actually signs and delivers a Deed, he is legally on title.

If a person is on the deed (and they are alive) or has any interest in the property, they must join in the listing and sale contract. A contract can be binding against those who do sign even if all the necessary parties did not sign. Suppose A, B, and C own a property but only A and B sign the contract. At closing C refuses to cooperate. The buyer could collect damages from A and B because they cannot deliver clear title without C's signature on the Deed.

DEPOSIT

Never accept a post-dated check. If you are to hold a check, be sure to include clause [22]. If a Note is used [25] - [26], be sure the buyer pays it when due [23]. If the buyer does not pay the note or the deposit check bounces, notify all parties immediately.

PROPERTY

Ask to check the seller's deed, survey or other document to be sure the legal description and names are correct. Watch out for "less and except" provisions in the seller's Deed, such as, "Less and except 20 feet on the West side of Rt. 50 conveyed to the state for highway widening." Don't obligate the seller to convey more than he owns.

Also be on the lookout for additional rights conveying with the property such as, "together with the right to use the 20 foot access road" or "together with Parking Space 314."

CHATTELS/EQUIPMENT

The difference between real property with fixtures, (that convey) and personal property (that does not convey) is not clear, nor well understood. Technically a "fixture" is anything permanently attached that can not be removed without damage. Don't take chances. List everything that conveys. It is not a good idea to refer back to a multiple listing printout, unless you attach a copy to the contract.

When listing or showing property for sale, the seller should remove anything that will not convey or carefully mark it.

CHECK THE LIST OF EQUIPMENT AND CHATTELS CAREFULLY! If something is in the listing, it is offered for sale. If it is not in the contract, it is not sold. If the buyer forgets to list the washer/dryer in his offer, the seller will be justified is saying it does not convey. Watch out for rented items such as water softeners or TV dishes.

Conversely, if an item is in the contract but not in the listing, the seller is obligated to deliver it even if that means buying a new one. The buyer could add and expect a washer/dryer when none was offered or present in the property.

Some particular problem items include: chandeliers, fireplace equipment and inserts, bars, burglar alarms, ceiling fans, water softeners, and garage door openers. At least once a year, we find a washer/dryer in the contract when none was included in the listing or vice versa.

If an item is to convey "AS IS," be sure to designate it as such in the contract. Humidifiers are a good example. If you leave the humidifier out of the contract because it doesn't work, the buyer may say it is part of the heating system. Then it is covered by a contract provision that the heating system will be in working order at the time of settlement. If you list it specifically, "AS IS," there is no ambiguity.

Accurately describe everything in the listing and the contract. Is it really a heat-pump or an electric furnace, continuous cleaning oven or self cleaning? If you advertise "hardwood floors," do they exist in the whole house or just parts? Is it wall-to-wall carpet or a large area rug?

PRICE

Offers and counter-offers written on the same form can be illegible and invite math errors. This is also true of reproduced or faxed forms. Don't be reluctant to take out a fresh new form and start over.

FINANCING

Be sure everyone understands any financing contingency and its limits. Can the buyer change financing and how will this impact the seller?

Be precise describing loan terms. Avoid the ambiguous phrase "best prevailing rate at the time of settlement."

SETTLEMENT DATE

Contracts provide a settlement date but many are flexible to extend that date if there are problems. Examples could be delays in the buyer's financing or difficulty with the title work or survey. To provide a definite cutoff, use [88]. "Time is of the essence" is a legal term meaning the timing really is material and important.

APPRAISAL CONTINGENCIES

Appraisal contingencies usually provide the buyer an option to go ahead in spite of a low appraisal. Be sure he must exercise the option promptly or the seller will be uncertain for an unreasonable period. For the same reason, an appeal of the appraisal should require the approval of both parties. [43].

Be careful changing appraisal provisions with VA or FHA loans. Government regulations require specific language. VA or FHA may decline the loan if the contract does not conform.

POSSESSION DATE

Usually, the seller delivers possession at settlement. Handle Pre and Post Occupancy agreements in writing at contract presentation, if possible. See [80] - [82].

LOAN APPLICATION

Most contracts contain a financing contingency. They impose a duty on the buyer to diligently pursue his loan application. Failure to do so is default. The buyer might also be in default if he misstates income or expenses or quits his job. See [40].

Many contracts require the buyer to apply to several different lenders if one rejects him. That process could take months and lead nowhere. It usually works to the seller's disadvantage. An alternative gives the seller an option to cancel the contract unless the buyer produces a loan commitment within a given time. See [35] and [37].

PROPERTY EQUIPMENT CONDITION

Practices vary in different areas but property condition is always a major concern and a fertile source of complaints. Many agents encourage sellers to hire a home inspector at the time of listing. A clean inspection is positive advertising. If the inspection reveals problems, the seller can take the appropriate remedial action before it becomes an issue and the buyer starts demanding adjustments. Buyers would always be well advised to hire a professional home inspector.

Many contracts provide that the property is sold "as is," except for limited warranties on equipment and appliances.

In many states, the seller is under no obligation to disclose defects although he may not actively conceal them or lie if questioned. Virginia is an example of a "caveat emptor" (buyer beware) state with a Seller Disclosure Form warning the buyer to make his own inspections and inquiries.

Other areas provide full or limited seller disclosure. Buyers should be cautious about a seller's disclosure. Not only is the seller motivated to shade the truth, the seller's disclosure can only be to the best of his knowledge and belief. The seller may not be aware of defects. Only a foolish buyer would rely on the uninformed seller.

A real estate agent is advised not to make any representations to the buyer or conduct any inspections, including the pre-settlement walk-through, on behalf of the buyer. To do so, invites trouble.

WELL AND SEPTIC INSPECTIONS

Lenders often demand these inspections as a condition of the loan. A septic inspection usually requires the property be occupied for 30 days prior to an inspection. Therefore, order an inspection before the seller vacates. The number of bedrooms and appliances represented must conform to the system's design regardless of the seller's assurance there have been no problems. If you do the inspections when the house is put on the market, it will allow time to correct any defects. [76] & [77].

TERMITE INSPECTION

Termite and wood-boring insect inspections may not be required by law, but can be part of the contract or lender requirements. The seller will want to limit the inspection to the house and not include fences and sheds. FHA and VA require repair of old damage even if no active infestation exists. [75].

REPAIRS

Be certain any required repairs are well defined. Home inspection contingencies should give the seller an option whether or not to make repairs. Many contracts require the seller to comply with all lender, FHA, VA, Well, Septic, Termite requirements without limit. Clause [86] protects the seller from unreasonable or excessive demands.

Avoid surprises! Get a home inspection before the house goes on the market.

DAMAGE, RISK OF LOSS, INSURANCE

These provisions determine when the risk of loss passes from the seller to the buyer. The seller should not cancel his insurance policy until the sales proceeds are in hand. Be sure the purchaser has an insurance policy and paid receipt at closing.

Condominiums include insurance in the condominium fee. However, that insurance only covers the building and does not protect the owner against individual liability or loss of personal property. The master condominium policy may also not cover appliances damaged in a fire, carpet replacement and interior walls. Advise the buyer to contact an insurance agent, preferably the agent who insures the condominium. If the same insurance company insurance both the owner and the condominium, there should be no gaps in the coverage.

Check with the lender several days before settlement for any specific insurance requirements. Many states do not recognize binders and lenders insist on a paid up policy. Some will accept a full guaranteed replacement cost policy. Others insist that the policy be for the full loan amount, even if that exceeds the value of the insured improvements. For graduated payment or negative amortization mortgages the insurance required might be equal to the maximum indebtedness.

PRORATIONS

Expenses of ownership are divided as of the settlement date. The seller should fill the oil tank and receive reimbursement from the purchaser. The seller will pay his portion of taxes, interest, association fees, etc. The seller should provide a letter that any homeowner association or condominium fees are current. If the sale includes a lease, see [78].

FEES

Be sure everyone agrees on the allocation of lender and settlement fees. Clauses [55]-[59] minimize confusion.

SIGNATURES

All parties must sign. Be very careful using powers of attorney. Most states require a licensed attorney at law to prepare a power of attorney. Many states limit use of powers of attorney and do not permit them for signing deeds. Lenders may have their own specific forms and will always want to review a proposed form before settlement.

Be sure to leave a copy of the contract or any amendments with the person signing and promptly deliver the fully ratified contract to all parties. Delivery is essential as an offer may be withdrawn by the receiving party if it is not delivered.

Many states adhere to the Statute of Frauds – a contract for the sale of real estate must be in writing. A Contract can not be enforced against a party unless you have a copy that he signed. A party may withdraw an offer or counter-offer until acceptance is delivered.

SECTION TWO - SUGGESTED CONTRACT CLAUSES

Defined terms are a convenient shortcut. Words like Property, Contract, Delivery, Ratification and Agent. A defined term is capitalized. These clauses assume certain defined terms. If your contract form does not define these terms you will need to write out a definition or fill in the appropriate information. Clauses [18]- [21] contain several suggested defined terms.

ADDENDUM FORMAT

An addendum is an addition to the basic contract. It can modify or add terms to the contract either before or after the parties agree on the basic terms. When it comes after the original contract it is sometimes called an amendment.

[1] Basic Addendum Format

This is an Addendum to the Contract between the parties dated _____ for the Property located at: (address).

In consideration of the mutual terms in this addendum and to further the Contract terms, the parties agree as follows:

(insert appropriate provisions or changes)

All parties have Ratified this addendum at (date)(time). Any time deadlines begin as of this Ratification.

As evidence of their agreement, all parties have signed below.

(Add signature lines for all Purchasers and Sellers. Agents or brokers should sign if they signed the Contract or if terms in the addendum affect them)

AGENTS LIABILITY/DUAL AGENCY

Clause [2] is a disclosure. It protects the agent from a claim that the parties did not understand or were not alerted to a potential problem. It could be modified to protect a buyer or seller disclosing adverse information.

Section Three of this book discusses the issue of dual agency. Many states have enacted legislation requiring a disclosure similar to [3] before an agent shows a potential purchaser property.

When the agent needs to disclose a possible dual agency relationship and obtain permission from the parties to proceed, use [4].

[2] Limit on Agents Liability

Purchaser and Seller acknowledge the Agents have presented them with a brief explanation of (the potential problem). The Agents have advised them of their right to seek advice from their own attorney, inspector, accountant or other professional. The Purchaser and Seller accept this disclosure and agree they will not make any claims against the Agents, or the Agent's company, whether or not they have actually sought such advice.

[3] Seller's Agent Agency Disclosure to a Purchaser

My Company, (insert company name), and myself, (insert your name), will be acting as agents of the seller and as such owe a duty of loyalty and faithfulness to the Seller. As seller's agents, we do not represent you, the purchaser.

An agent representing the seller can furnish many valuable services, make recommendations to you, assist you in locating suitable property and financing, assist you in submitting an offer to purchase, and provide information about the settlement process. Agents representing the seller must respond truthfully to questions asked of them, must disclose material facts, must submit all offers and communicate to the seller all information you have given them.

Agents who represent purchasers are called Buyer Agents. If you wish to enter into a Buyer Agency arrangement you should do so before you are shown property. If you need legal or tax advice, you should consult an attorney or financial professional.

We acknowledge that we have read and understand this disclosure.

(Add signature lines for purchaser and agent)

[4] Dual Agency Disclosure

NOTICE TO BUYER AND SELLER AND CONSENT AGREEMENT

This Notice and Consent Agreement is acknowledged and agreed to this _____day of _____, 20__ by and between:

_____ (Purchaser),
_____ (Seller),
_____ (Listing Agent and Company) and
_____ (Selling Agent and Company).

This Notice and Consent Agreement alerts all parties to this transaction of a potential conflict of interest. The parties acknowledge this potential conflict and have taken the steps they feel appropriate to protect themselves. The Agents have advised them to seek advice from their own attorney or other legal representative(s) regarding this transaction. Whether or not they have actually sought such advice, Purchaser and Seller agree to make no claim against the Listing or Selling Agents or their companies or brokers.

As agents of the seller, we owe a duty of loyalty and faithfulness to the seller. In representing the seller, the agents are obligated to bring the seller the highest possible offer under the best possible terms. A conflict of interest may interfere with that duty.

In this particular transaction, there is a real or potential conflict of interest because: (list the reason - examples include)

The Selling Agent or a relative or close friend of the Selling Agent is also the Purchaser.

The Listing Agent or a relative or close friend of the Listing Agent is also the Purchaser.

The Purchaser is affiliated with or employed by the Listing or Selling Company.

The Seller can elect not to negotiate with the Purchaser as a result of this potential conflict and the Seller is advised to seek other representation if he continues negotiation.

The Purchaser can elect not to negotiate with the Seller as a result of the potential conflict and is advised to seek other representation if he continues negotiation.

The parties acknowledge they have received a complete disclosure and have elected to proceed with this transaction notwithstanding a real or potential conflict of interest. If a commission is earned it may be shared by the Agents and their companies according to the listing agreement.

We acknowledge we have read and understand this disclosure.

(Add signature lines for all parties and agents)

BACK-UP CONTRACT OR OFFER

[5] Basic Back-Up Provision

This Contract is the first back-up contract or offer subject to a sale contract of (date) from Purchasers (name). It will become the primary contract or offer immediately upon written notification the first contract is no longer in effect. This Contract or offer terminates immediately upon settlement of the primary contract. The Purchaser may withdraw this back-up unilaterally any time before receipt of written notice from Seller that it is the prime contract. Any such withdrawal must be in writing and is effective when delivered to Seller's address or Agent. Withdrawal will cancel this Contract or offer with the deposit returned to the Purchaser.

The Sellers may modify or amend the primary contract without obtaining Purchaser's permission and must promptly notify Purchaser of any modifications.

BUYER AGENCY

Refer to Section Three of this book for a discussion of buyer agency and the dangers of undisclosed dual agency.

Buyer Agents should disclose their agency relationship with the Buyer immediately and often. The disclosure should be to all relevant parties including the other agents, the Seller and the settlement agent.

The following buyer agency forms assume the buyer agent can be affiliated with the listing company. Check the laws, regulations and practices in your area to confirm this is an acceptable practice.

The Buyer Agency Agreement in [6] calls for a non-refundable retainer fee. A retainer is not necessary to make the agreement binding and many buyer agents collect only a nominal fee, if any. In most jurisdictions, an agent can only receive compensation from the broker. Any retainer fee belongs to the broker not the individual agent. The fee is then subject the agent's commission agreement.

[6] "Buyer Agency" Exclusive Agreement to Represent Buyer

THIS AGREEMENT made as of _____, 20_____, between _____ ("Buyer") and _____ ("Buyer's Agent"), provides as follows:

1. Agreement to Retain The Buyer retains Buyer's Agent to locate property and to negotiate for Buyer's Purchase. Buyer has paid Buyer's Agent a NON-REFUNDABLE retainer fee of_____ Dollars ($_____). This fee is earned when paid and shall be a credit toward fees due under paragraph 5.

2. Term This Agreement shall be effective beginning on the date shown above and expiring at 11:59 p.m. on _____, 20____. This Agreement shall also apply to any property presented or described to Buyer by Buyer's Agent during the term of this Agreement when a contract is entered into within _____ days of the expiration date. The extension period shall not apply if the buyer enters into another Buyer Agent agreement with another real estate broker.

3. Buyer's Agent's Obligation Buyer's Agent agrees to work diligently to locate property acceptable to Buyer, and to negotiate as Buyer's agent on terms and conditions acceptable to Buyer.

4. Buyer's Agent Fees If, during the term of this Agreement, or within the extended period described in paragraph 3, Buyer enters into an agreement to Purchase any property, whether through the services of Buyer's Agent or otherwise, Buyer agrees to pay Buyer's Agent for his services compensation of _____. Any compensation paid to Buyer's Agent by the seller shall be a credit against this fee. Buyer's Agent makes no representation the Seller will always agree to pay the fee. Buyer acknowledges that the fee will be owed in full upon ratification of a contract.

5. Additional Terms

_____.

6. Buyer's Obligations   Buyer agrees to purchase property exclusively through Buyer's Agent during this Agreement period.   Buyer understands the Buyer's Agent's fee will be due if property is purchased through any source. The fee is compensation to Agent for time and effort expended as well as expertise, counseling and services in connection with the search for an acceptable property whether or not that search led to the property purchased. Buyer will comply with requests for financial data needed to fulfill the terms of any purchase agreement. Buyer will be available to view properties during Buyer's Agent's normal working hours. Buyer agrees that the information disclosed to Buyer's Agent by Buyer, including but not limited to the availability, terms, potential sellers and potential uses of property, is and will be disclosed to Buyer in confidence. Buyer will not disclose confidential information to anyone, except as necessary to effect the transactions contemplated by this Agreement. Buyer's Agent has the right to rely on the assurance of non-disclosure by Buyer.

7. Entire Agreement   This Agreement, any modifications signed by the parties, is the entire Exclusive Agreement between Buyer and Buyer's Agent and supersede any other written or oral agreements. This Agreement can be modified only by a writing signed by Buyer and Buyer's Agent.

8. Attorney's Fees The prevailing party shall be entitled to receive reasonable attorney's fees as set by the court or arbitrator in any proceeding to enforce this agreement.

9. Disclosure The Buyer's Agent may represent several buyers interested in the same property. Other agents, associated with the same company as Buyer's Agent, may represent sellers of property. If the same company represents both the buyer and seller, there are limits on that company's ability to represent either party. The agents may not disclose information obtained in a relationship of trust and confidence without prior written permission of the party adversely affected by the disclosure.

10. Definitions "Purchase" includes any purchase, option, exchange or lease of property or an agreement to do so. "Buyer" includes any affiliate, nominee or assignee of Buyer and any person acting on behalf of Buyer, either directly or indirectly.

This is an exclusive agreement. The Buyer's Agent will have earned a fee if the Buyer purchases any property from any source. Consult with the Buyer Agent before visiting any new or resale homes or contacting any owners or other agents.

WITNESS the following duly authorized signatures and seals:

(Add signature lines for all parties)

[7] Buyer Agent Fee Paid By Seller

Agents may need a clause to authorize payment of the Buyer Agent's Fee when property has not been listed in a multiple listing service that recognizes buyer agency. The following clause can also be modified to use when dealing with For Sale By Owner by eliminating reference to the listing company.

The parties acknowledge (Buyer Agent's Company) has acted as a compensated "Buyer Agent" and agent for the Purchaser and is not acting as an agent for the Seller or a sub-agent of the listing Broker. Seller agrees to pay on behalf of Buyer and authorizes the Listing Broker to pay the Buyer Agent a fee of $_____, at settlement.

Modifying the listing agreement - When property is listed for sale in a multiple listing service, the Listing Company offers agents affiliated with other companies an opportunity to sell it. These agents may represent either the buyer or the seller. Some agents affiliated with the Listing Company may represent buyers. Sellers should be cautious discussing the property with other agents as they may represent buyers.

[8] Buyer Agency Addendum to the Listing Agreement

The Listing Company is authorized to show the property and make it available to buyers and buyer's agents.

The Listing Company is authorized to pay a portion of the listing compensation to an agent representing a buyer.

An agent affiliated with the Listing Company may represent a buyer but only with the knowledge and consent of both the buyer and the seller. Even with consent, the Listing company is limited in its ability to represent one party against the other. Any information obtained from one party may not be revealed to the other without the written authorization of the party adversely affected by the disclosure.

[9] Disclosure that Buyer Agent is Affiliated with the Listing Company

The parties acknowledge that (agent's name) is affiliated with (Listing Company's name) but acting as a Buyer Agent representing the buyer in this transaction. The parties consent to this dual representation and understand that the Listing Company is limited in its ability to represent one party exclusively. Any information obtained from one party may not be revealed to the other without the written authorization of the party adversely affected by the disclosure.

CHATTELS/EQUIPMENT

Do not refer to the listing printout in the contract. Write out everything included in the sale. An item on the listing is offered for sale. If it is not in the contract, it is not sold.

Assume nothing. This is a major area of seller and purchaser disputes. If the seller can remove an item without causing permanent damage to the structure, it is personal property. It belongs to the seller under the laws of most states. List everything and be specific.

Problems: storm windows/doors, window fans and air conditioning units, electronic air filters, chandeliers, lights, fireplace inserts and equipment, carpet, curtains, drapes, rods, mirrors, doorbells, workbenches, bars, window locks, burglar alarms, garage door openers, door knockers, bookshelves, ceiling fans, water softeners, children's playhouses and swings, special landscape features.

In addition, you must be certain to describe the items accurately. Where are they located? How many? Will the seller replace any items? Is it a heat pump or electric furnace? Is the refrigerator frost free? Is the oven continuous cleaning or self cleaning?

If an item is to convey "as is," be sure to designate it as such in the contract. Humidifiers are a good example. If you leave one out of the contract because it doesn't work, the buyer may say it is part of the heating system and covered by the contract provision that the heating system will be in working order at the time of settlement. If you list it specifically, "as is," there is no ambiguity.

CLOSING COSTS

There is a great deal of confusion regarding the phrase "Seller to pay Closing Costs". Do closing costs include buy-down points, escrows, interest, reimbursement for credit reports and appraisals? Adding "except prepaid items" is of little help. How about mortgage insurance, optional owner's title insurance, subsidy points and additional attorney's fees for reviewing the contract or preparing a Power of Attorney? Suggest either a flat dollar credit [10] (preferred) or specific listing of items [11].

[10] Dollar Credit

Seller will credit purchaser, at closing, with $_____ toward the cash required for settlement to defray closing costs and related expenses as allowed by the Purchaser's lender. Any unused credit will be returned to the Seller.

[11] Credit for Listed Items

Seller will pay Purchaser's loan origination fee, up to _____ loan discount points, settlement attorney fees, title binder fees, mortgagee title insurance, recording fees and survey charges. (Select the appropriate items)

FINANCING COSTS SEE [55] - [59]

CONTINGENCIES

Improperly-worded contingencies can create legal problems. The contingency must be in an "if - when - then" proposition. If something happens or doesn't happen by a certain time, then what? Does the contingency expire and remove itself or does the contract cancel because the contingency was not removed?

The contingency should also make clear which party has the right to invoke it. Example - If a contract is contingent on the sale of the purchaser's house by a certain date and the date passes, then what? Can the seller do nothing and thereby extend the time forcing the purchaser to continue to market his house? Can the purchaser extend the time and force the seller to stay with the contract? Does the contract become non-contingent after the date passes or does the contract automatically die?

Given a choice, contingencies should require an affirmative act to keep the contract alive. The parties' acceptance is much stronger if supported by an affirmative act. It is dangerous to allow automatic removal of a contingency by the mere passage of time. The purchaser might claim the phone call the agent interpreted as healthy concern was actually a cancellation. The agent is then liable for not having followed through to cancel the contract. It is not practical for every contingency to follow this rule.

Whether you choose to have the contingency removed by the passage of time or require an affirmative act, you must keep careful track of the time periods. Don't lose rights because you forgot a deadline.

You might want to make a contingency removable by the party it benefits by notice and without the need for a contract amendment. Use this only when the contingency removed does not affect the other side. You can add Clause [12] to most contingencies but not the sale of home contingency [15].

[12] Unilateral Removal

The Purchaser/Seller may remove this contingency unilaterally, without cause, by written notice to the other parties to this contract.

[13] General Purpose Contingency

This contract is contingent until (time, date) upon the (Purchaser or Seller) obtaining a (bridge loan, gift letter, trade agreement, engineer's approval, release from prior contract, attorney review, spouse's inspection, confirmation of zoning, confirmation of permitted uses, etc.) at their own expense and with due diligence. This contract cancels unless the (Purchaser or Seller) gives written notice removing this contingency before the deadline.

[14] Kick-Out Clause (General)

Seller will continue to market the Property. Should Seller receive an acceptable offer before Purchaser removes this contingency, the Purchaser will have (hours/days) from the time of written notification to remove the contingency. In the event the Purchaser does not remove the contingency in writing within the time given, then this contract cancels with all parties released and the deposit refunded.

[15] Contingency for Sale of Purchaser's Property

The Sales Contract is contingent upon the sale of "Purchaser's Property" located at _____ and this Contract is canceled at 9:00 p.m. on (date) unless Purchaser either:

(1) Accepts a bona fide non-contingent (except for financing) contract for the sale of Purchaser's Property to settle on or before the settlement date of this Contract; and delivers to Seller or Listing Agent a copy of such contract with an amendment signed by Purchaser removing this contingency;

OR

(2) Delivers to the Seller or Listing Agent:

(a) an amendment signed by Purchaser removing the contingency; and

(b) evidence of funds necessary for Purchaser to perform under the terms of this Contract; and

(c) a lender's written opinion letter substantiating Purchaser's financial ability to perform without selling or leasing Purchaser's Property, together with copies of any other special documentation the lender requires (for example, signed gift letter or bank statements evidencing funds to close).

If the evidence provided is reasonably sufficient to indicate Purchaser's ability to perform under the terms of this Contract, Seller agrees to sign the amendment removing this contingency. If the evidence is not reasonably sufficient, then Seller shall give Purchaser a written statement setting forth the reasons, and cancel this Contract with the deposit refunded to Purchaser. In either case, Seller agrees to respond in writing within 2 Days.

Purchaser shall immediately:

(1) offer Purchaser's Property for sale at a price not to exceed _____ ($_____); and

(2) actively market the Property with a licensed real estate broker for the entire term of this Contract.

Optional: Add [16]

[16] Sale of Home Kick-out Clause

Seller may continue to offer this Property for sale until the parties remove this Contingency. If the Seller accepts a backup offer, Seller will notify the Selling Agent and deliver written notice to Purchaser's address at _____. The Purchaser will then have until 9:00 p.m. on the

_____ business day after delivery of the notice to remove this Contingency as set forth above or this Contract cancels with the deposit refunded to the Purchaser.

[17] Coinciding Settlement - may be added to [15]

Settlement on the Purchaser's Property located at _____ must occur before, or coincide with, settlement of this Contract. Purchaser may not delay settlement under this Contract more than _____ days after the settlement date specified, without Seller's written consent. (Add either option 1 or 2)

OPTION 1 - Purchaser must proceed to settlement within the time frame of this Contract or be in default. The provision calling for coinciding settlements is for convenience only and not a contingency. Failure to settle will be a default.

OPTION 2 - This provision creates a contingency. The Seller may cancel this Contract if Purchaser's property does not settle within the time frame stated, as extended by Seller.

Assume the Purchaser removes the contingency on the sale of his property and elects Option 1. Assume also the loan commitment requires sale of the Purchaser's property. If it does not settle, the Purchaser will not be able to close with the Seller and is in default.

OTHER CONTINGENCIES:

Appraisal [44] & [45}
Credit Report [62]
Equity Sharing [34]
Home Inspection [71]
New Home [79]
New Loan [35] & [37]
Preliminary Loan Approval [35]
Review of Homeowner or Condominium Association Documents [70]
Sale of Seller Held Note [63]
Study Contingency [89]
Survey [90] & [91]

DEFINED TERMS

Defined terms make drafting easier and more concise because we do not need to describe the term each time we use it. Defined terms are capitalized. The following definitions are not from a dictionary. They are agreed contract terms and only apply if they are part of the contract.

[18] Days

Days mean calendar days. To compute time, the first Day shall be the Day following an event and the period shall end at 9 P.M. on the Day specified.

Example: A three Day notice is delivered Monday. Tuesday is the first day and the notice expires on Thursday at 9 P.M.

[19] Delivery or Delivered

Delivery or Delivered means to provide a document to the address specified for Notice either by hand carrying or sending it by a service that produces a receipt. The time of Delivery is when received at that address.

[20] Notice

Notice shall be effective when Delivered in writing to (a) the Seller at _____ ; (b) the Purchaser at: _____ .

Note: Agents should avoid using their address for Delivery as Delivery starts the clock on many contingencies and notices. You want the clock to start when the item actually reaches the buyer or seller, not when it is dropped off at the agent's office.

[21] Ratification and Date of Ratification

Ratification means final acceptance, by all parties, in writing, of all the Contract terms. The Date of Ratification is the Day this occurs. It is not the Day of expiration or removal of all contingencies.

For short sales you might consider adding:

This Contract is subject to third party approval and is not deemed "ratified" until written third party approval is Delivered to all parties.

DEPOSITS

Never use a post-dated check. Use a deposit note if the purchaser's funds will be coming later. [25] [26]

Don't hold a check unless all parties have agreed in writing. [22]

[22] Check Holding

The parties agree that the Agent/Seller will hold the deposit check until (written third party approval, date or contingency removal), at which time the Agent/Seller will promptly deposit the check.

[23] Failure to Pay Deposit

Seller may declare this contract in default if purchaser fails to redeem the deposit note or if the deposit check is not honored.

[24] If Agent/Broker Does Not Hold The Deposit

Buyer and Seller acknowledge that _____ will hold the earnest money deposit. Neither Agent/Broker nor their company will have any liability for the deposit.

DEPOSIT NOTE

Sometimes the deposit will take the form of a Note payable on the expiration of a contingency or a period of time. Be sure the Purchaser signs the deposit note and it has a definite due date. "Due at settlement" is not a definite due date. The note does not necessarily need to provide for interest.

The Note should contain a provision that the failure to pay when due is a default under the contract. Many states have held that without this provision, failure to pay is not a default of the Contract but only gives the Seller the right to sue to collect the deposit. [23]

[25] Note for Deposit

Purchaser has delivered a negotiable promissory note due on (date) as a deposit. A copy is attached to this contract.

[26] Deposit Note

For value received, the undersigned, jointly and severally (if more than one) promise to pay to the order of (Agent or Seller) at such place as the holder may designate, the principal sum of $_____ without interest. After default, interest shall be charged at the rate of 1 ½% per month (18% APR).

This Note is a deposit under the attached Contract. This Note shall be due and payable (within _____ days or expiration of the _____ contingency as stated in the Contract).

If the Purchaser does not pay this Note when due, Agent's sole liability and responsibility, shall be to notify the Seller or Listing Agent, in writing, within 24 hours.

Upon failure of the Purchaser to pay as required, the Seller shall have the option to declare the Contract breached and pursue all legal and equitable remedies or to declare the Contract canceled.

The Purchasers agree to pay all costs and attorney's fees should it become necessary to place this Note in the hands of an attorney for collection or to protect the interest of the holder as provided in the Contract.

Date: _____ _____(Seal)

       Purchaser(s)

SEEN & AGREED TO:

Date: _____ _____(Seal)

       Seller(s)

DOWN PAYMENT

The Purchaser's down payment is the difference between any financing and the contract sales price. It is different than the deposit - the amount the Purchaser tenders with the contract. The down payment includes the deposit and can take the form of cash (certified or cashier's check) or other consideration. The other consideration could take several forms itself, such as other property. Exchanges of property may qualify for special tax deferred treatment. Section Three and [92] - [94] cover tax deferred exchanges.

When the down payment is to take the form of a Note, held by the Purchaser but made by another party, use Clause [29] for unsecured Notes or Clause [30] for secured Notes.

[27] Personal Property as the Down Payment

As part (or all) of the down payment, Purchaser agrees to convey to Seller, at the time of settlement, the following (auto, farm equipment, etc.) subject to the following liens, if any: (name of lien holder) having an outstanding balance of $_____ payable $_____ per month until (date) when the full balance shall be due and payable. The total credit against the downpayment shall be $_____ based on these figures and should the outstanding balance change before settlement, the credit against the down payment shall adjust accordingly. The (Purchaser or Seller) shall pay all costs of the transfer, including sales taxes.

Seller has inspected the property and agrees to accept it (as-is condition or subject to the following repairs which Purchaser agrees to make: _____).

OPTIONAL: Purchaser reserves the right the substitute cash at settlement instead of transfer of the property.

[28] Real Property as the Down Payment

As part (or all) of the down payment, Purchaser agrees to convey to Seller, at the time of settlement, the following real property: (legal description and list of chattels to convey) subject to the following liens, if any: (name of lien holder) having an outstanding balance of $_____ payable $_____ per month until (date) when the full balance shall be due and payable. The total credit against the downpayment shall be $_____ based on these figures, and should the outstanding balance change prior to settlement, the credit against the down payment adjust accordingly. The general terms of sale shall be the same as those set forth in this contract except where in conflict with this paragraph. *

Seller has inspected the property to be transferred and agrees to accept it (in as-is condition or subject to the following repairs which Purchaser agrees to make:_____). Equipment, termite, well and septic warranties (are or are not) intended to apply to the transferred property.

OPTIONAL: Purchaser reserves the right to substitute cash instead of the transfer.

* NOTE: By incorporating all the terms of the printed contract into the transfer agreement, the Purchaser becomes liable for all the warranties and responsibilities that the Seller has to him on the primary contract. Examples, where applicable, would be the need for well, septic and termite inspections as well as the requirement that all heating, electrical, plumbing, etc. be in working order.

[29] Another's Unsecured Note as Down Payment

As part (or all) of the down payment, Purchaser agrees to endorse to Seller, at the time of settlement, an unsecured Note made by (name of note maker). The Note has an outstanding balance of $_____ . A copy of the Note is attached. The total credit against the downpayment shall be $_____ based on these figures and should the outstanding balance change before settlement, the credit against the downpayment shall adjust accordingly.

Purchaser will endorse the Note with full recourse and warrant that the Note is not in default and that he knows of no defenses, set-offs or claims against the Note.

OPTIONAL: Purchaser reserves the right to substitute cash in the amount of the agreed credit instead of endorsing the Note to Seller.

[30] Another's Secured Note as Down Payment

As part (or all) of the down payment, Purchaser agrees to endorse to Seller, at the time of settlement, the Note made by (name of note maker) secured by a first/second lien against real property known as: (address or legal description) and subject to the following other liens, if any: (name of lien holder and amount, monthly payments and due date). The Note has an outstanding balance of $_____. A copy of the Note and Mortgage or Deed of Trust is attached. The total credit against the downpayment shall be $_____ based on these figures and should the outstanding balance change before settlement, the credit against the down payment shall adjust accordingly.

Purchaser will endorse the Note with full recourse and warrant that the Note is not in default and that he knows of no defenses, set-offs or claims against the Note and that he knows of no liens except as disclosed and no defenses to the security instrument. The (Purchaser or Seller) shall pay the cost of recording an assignment of the security instrument.

OPTIONAL: Purchaser reserves the right to substitute cash instead of endorsing the Note to Seller.

EQUIPMENT AND PROPERTY CONDITION

This is a major area of after-contract disputes and misunderstandings. A home warranty or professional home inspection can help. Clause [71] is a home inspection contingency.

The practice regarding Seller's warranties and representations varies. No matter what standard your state applies, both buyer and seller must understand what to expect. The clauses below are two possibilities.

[31] "As Is" with Appliance Warranty

Purchaser has thoroughly inspected the property and accepts its present physical condition ("as is") except as specifically provided otherwise in this contract. Seller warrants that all appliances, heating and cooling equipment, plumbing and electrical systems will be in normal working order at the time of settlement or occupancy, whichever first occurs. Seller will deliver the property in its present physical condition, broom clean and free of trash or abandoned items. Purchaser and Purchaser's representatives shall have reasonable access prior to settlement to conduct a final inspection.

[32] "As Is" Without Any Warranty

Purchaser accepts the property sold in strictly "as is" condition without warranty of any kind, either as to the structure or any of the appliances conveyed or any of the systems within the property, such as heating, cooling, electrical and plumbing. Purchaser has assured himself that the property is suitable for his particular needs. Purchaser accepts all defects known or unknown.

[33] Special Clause for Air Conditioning

In the event weather conditions make testing the air conditioning systems impractical, Seller shall either supply Purchaser with an inspection report from a licensed air conditioner supplier or repair firm, certifying that the system is in operating condition, or the Seller shall continue to remain liable until the weather warms sufficiently to test the system.

Alternate:

The seller will provide a home warranty or service contract from a recognized source and agrees to pay any deductible should the air conditioner fail to operate normally for six months following closing.

This clause is actually a restatement of the existing law if the Seller has warranted the cooling system will be in working order at the time of settlement. He will continue to be liable for its proper operation until the following season unless he can prove it was operating properly at the time of settlement. An inspection report or warranty takes the Seller off the hook immediately.

EQUITY SHARING & JOINT OWNERSHIP

Always recommend a written agreement when two or more unmarried parties buy property. Equity sharing or joint ownership can be of substantial benefit to both the occupant and the investor. Section Three contains an article on equity sharing or joint ownership. In many instances, the occupant has not had an opportunity to come to a full agreement with the investor and needs a contingency to work out the details. Section Four contains a sample form.

[34] Equity Sharing Contingency

Purchaser intends to enter into an Equity Sharing or Joint Ownership Agreement. This Contract shall be contingent upon such an Agreement. If the Purchaser has not removed this contingency in writing by (date) the Contract shall

be in full force and effect

OR

cancel with the deposit refunded upon the execution of appropriate release documents.

To remove this contingency, Purchaser and Seller must agree on Purchaser's ability to qualify for loan approval and close.

FINANCING

Financing has always been a part of the sale. Many loan programs are completely new and foreign to the buyer. Loan terms are a major source of misunderstanding. Often the loan that was available when the contract was written is not available by the time of settlement. Therefore, there must be some flexibility in any financing contingency.

[35] Contingency on Preliminary Loan Approval

This contract is contingent until (time/date) upon Purchaser's Delivering to Seller a lender's preliminary loan qualification letter stating, based on the information supplied by the Purchaser, review of the Purchaser's credit report and subject to final verification, the financing described is available to the Purchaser. If the Purchaser does not deliver this letter by the deadline, at Seller's option, this contract shall be canceled and the deposit refunded.

[36] Alternate Loan Application

The Purchaser shall have the right to apply for other financing for which he is reasonably qualified; provided, there are no additional expenses to Seller and no delay of settlement. The Purchaser must apply for a program for which he is reasonably qualified. The Purchaser and Seller must agree on an amendment to the sales contract changing financing or the Purchaser waives the benefit of any financing contingency.

[37] Loan Application and Financing Contingency

Purchaser agrees to make written loan application within five (5) business days following Ratification of this Contract. If Purchaser's loan application is rejected or withdrawn, then, with Seller's approval, the Purchaser, will make application to one additional qualified lender to obtain financing. This additional application must be at Seller's request and only with Seller's permission. If the purchaser can not obtain financing or assumption approval, this Contract shall cancel with the deposit refunded to the Purchaser.

Note: You may also wish to add Clause [40].

[38] Adjustable Rate Loan (also used for assumption)

The financing terms set forth are for the first adjustment period only and will be subject to change. A summary of the loan terms is as follows:

Initial Interest Rate _____%
Interest Adjusted Every _____ Months
Payment Adjusted Every _____ Months
Index (One year T-Bill) Margin (2 points)
Maximum Change Per Year ____% (or no limit)
Maximum Rate Over Life of Loan ____% (or no limit)
Loan Term _____ years
Negative Amortization? Yes/No

[39] Graduated Payment Loan (also used for assumption)

The financing terms set forth are for the first payment period only and will be subject to change. A summary of those changes is as follows:

First Year Payment _____/month
Payment Increase _____% per year
Payments Increase for _____ years
Payment at End of Increases _____/month
Loan Term _____ years
Negative Amortization? Yes/No
Total Amount of Negative Amortization $_____

[40] Financing Duties

The Purchaser must diligently apply for and pursue loan approval and cooperate fully with the lender to obtain financing. Any failure to cooperate or other actions taken by the Purchaser to hinder loan approval shall be a default by the Purchaser. Other defaults by the Purchaser include:

(a) failure to lock in the interest rate or program and the Purchaser no longer qualifies, rates change or the program is no longer available, or

(b) applying for financing other than as specified in the Contract, without Sellers permission, and failing to obtain financing, or

(c) failing to have the funds required to settle, including any gift letter proceeds, or

(d) doing anything following Ratification of this Contract that prevents Purchaser from qualifying.

[41] Interest Rate Changes

If the interest rate changes before settlement or the Purchaser is unable to obtain a loan as described, then the Purchaser agrees to accept the Lender's rate at the time of settlement so long as the Lender determines that the Purchaser qualifies for the new loan terms.

Note: The Purchaser may also wish to add Clause [42]

[42] Maximum Interest Rate

Provided, if Purchaser is unable to obtain a rate of less than _____% per annum, Purchaser may cancel this contract and receive a refund of the deposit.

[43] Appraisal Appeal

Appeal of the appraisal value shall be at the request of (Seller, Purchaser, Seller or Purchaser, only Seller and Purchaser).

[44] Appraisal Contingency Tied to Financing

(Do not use with VA or FHA financing. VA and FHA have their own requirements and you should use the latest VA/FHA addendum available from your lender.

If the financing specified in this Contract is not possible because of the lender's appraisal and the parties are unable to agree on terms to satisfy the requirements, then it shall first be Seller's option to lower the purchase price to permit the financing. If Seller does not exercise that option, the Purchaser may elect to accept the lower appraised value and loan amount or declare the contract canceled. All elections must be by written contract amendment and made within 3 days of written notice or this Contract cancels with the deposit returned to the Purchaser.

[45] Appraisal Contingency Tied to Price

This Contract is contingent on receiving a lender's appraisal of not less than the full contract price. If the lender's appraisal is less than the contract price, then it shall first be Seller's option to accept the appraisal as the contract price. If Seller does not exercise that option, and the parties are unable to agree on other terms, the Purchaser may elect to remove this contingency and accept the contract price or declare the contract canceled. All elections must be by written contract amendment and made within 3 days of written notice or this Contract cancels with the deposit returned to the Purchaser.

FINANCING, ASSUMPTIONS

You must state all the loan terms accurately in the contract. Be careful of changing loan balances as they affect the down payment amount. This is primarily the listing agent's responsibility. See clause [52] to freeze the down payment.

Any variation between the contract and the actual assumption terms is grounds for cancellation. Disclose pre-payment penalties, payment variations, balloons and mortgage insurance requirements. VA and FHA assumption guidelines vary depending on the age of the loan. Get a letter, in advance, from the lender setting forth any charges and terms of an assumption.

If you need a substitution of VA eligibility, or release of liability, you must negotiate it into the contract. It is too late to think about them later.

A Purchaser should be careful about waiving the protection of a survey, title insurance or termite, well and septic inspections just because there is no new lender requiring them. The Agent should be very careful deleting these items from a contract as the Purchaser may look to the Agent later if problems arise.

The smart Seller may want a credit report from the Purchaser before he settles on an assumption. See clause [62].

If the Seller is taking back a note, the amount of the note depends on the exact loan balance assumed. If the down payment is firm and the note adjusts, use clause [53]. If the note is firm and the down payment adjusts, use clause [54].

[46] Limit on Costs

If the lender refuses to allow assumption of the loan under the terms stated or charges Purchaser more than $_____ or Seller more than $_____, then the effected party may promptly either a) elect to declare the contract canceled with the deposit refunded or b) waive this requirement and accept the lender's terms.

[47] - [50] Release of Liability and/or Substitution of VA Entitlement

Note: The release of liability and substitution of entitlement are two separate issues. There can be a release without a substitution. The seller's VA eligibility remains restricted unless there is a substitution.

VA loans originated after March 1, 1988 contain a due on sale clause and only a qualified buyer, who makes application and pays the required fees, can assume one. However, present VA regulations specifically allow use of a contract for deed or installment sale arrangement to transfer property without formal assumption. Check for the most recent fees and policies. There is no restriction on assuming a VA loan originated before March 1, 1988.

See Section Three of this book for articles on VA loans and contract for deed financing.

[47] Release of Liability Without Substitution of Entitlement for a VA Loan with a Due On Sale Clause

This property is sold subject to an existing VA loan and settlement is subject to VA approval of the Purchaser and written release of liability of the Seller to the VA, without the substitution of the Purchaser's VA entitlement for that of the Seller. Purchaser agrees to make application to the VA (or lender) within 5 days of ratification of this Contract. If VA declines to approve the Purchaser and release the Seller from liability, within 45 days, this Contract cancels with the deposit refunded to the Purchaser.

[48] Release of Liability Without Substitution of Entitlement for a VA Loan without a Due On Sale Clause

This property is sold subject to an existing VA loan and sale is subject to VA approval of the Purchaser and written release of liability of the Seller to the VA, without the substitution of the Purchaser's VA entitlement for that of the Seller. Purchaser agrees to make application to the VA (or lender) within 5 days of ratification of this Contract. If VA declines to approve the Purchaser and release the Seller from liability, within 45 days, the Seller shall have the option to waive the requirement and proceed to settlement or declare this contract canceled.

OPTIONAL: If the Purchaser has not obtained full approval for release before settlement, the Seller may elect to hold a wrap-around Deed of Trust or mortgage due and payable in full one year from the date of settlement or upon rejection of the Purchaser by VA. The Purchaser will assume the existing loan directly and the Seller will release the wrap-around obligation when the Purchaser completes the release of Seller's liability. All parties agree to cooperate in order to accomplish this provision. Any additional charges will be paid by (Purchaser or Seller, or divided equally).

[49] Release of Liability and Substitution of Entitlement for a VA Loan with a Due on Sale Clause

This property is sold subject to an existing VA loan and settlement is subject to VA approval of the Purchaser and written release of liability of the Seller to the VA, and the substitution of the Purchaser's VA entitlement for that of the Seller. Purchaser agrees to make application within 5 days of ratification of this Contract. If VA declines to release the Seller from liability and reinstate the Seller's VA entitlement, in full, within 45 days, this contract cancels with the Deposit returned to the Purchaser.

[50] Release of Liability With Substitution of Entitlement for a VA Loan without a Due On Sale Clause

This property is sold subject to an existing VA loan and sale is subject to VA approval of the Purchaser and written release of liability of the Seller to the VA, and the substitution of the Purchaser's VA entitlement for that of the Seller. Purchaser agrees to make application within 5 days of ratification of this Contract. If VA declines to approve the Purchaser and release the Seller from liability and reinstate the Seller's VA eligibility in full, within 45 days, the Seller shall have the option to waive the requirement and proceed to settlement or declare this contract canceled.

OPTIONAL: If the Purchaser has not obtained full approval for release and substitution before settlement, the Seller may elect to hold a wrap-around Deed of Trust or mortgage due and payable in full one year from the date of settlement or upon rejection of the Purchaser by VA. The Purchaser will assume the existing loan directly and the Seller will release the wrap-around obligation when the Purchaser completes the release and substitution. All parties agree to cooperate in order to accomplish this provision. Any additional charges will be paid by (Purchaser or Seller, or divided equally).

[51] One Time Limit on VA Assumption

Seller has agreed to allow only the Purchaser to assume his VA loan and Purchaser agrees that no other party may assume or taken subject to the loan unless Seller has received a full release of liability and/or reinstatement of VA entitlement. The settlement agent is directed to place this covenant in the Deed of Conveyance to Purchaser.

[52] Down Payment Firm, Price Adjusts

The down payment in this contract is firm and the Purchaser shall pay no more than that amount over the balance of the financing being assumed and any seller held financing. The sales price may be adjusted lower but not higher so that the cash down payment remains the same.

OPTIONAL: If the adjustment of the sale price exceeds $_____, either party may cancel this Contract with the deposit returned to the Purchaser.

[53] Down Payment Firm, Seller Held Note Adjusts

The down payment and price stated in this contract are firm. The amount of the seller held note may be adjusted lower or higher so that the cash down payment remains the same.

OPTIONAL: If the adjustment of the seller held note exceeds $_____ , either party may cancel this Contract with the deposit returned to the Purchaser.

[54] Down Payment Adjusts, Seller Held Note Firm

The price and note amount stated in this contract are firm. The amount of the down payment may be adjusted so that the note amount remains as stated.

OPTIONAL: If the adjustment of the down payment exceeds $_____ , either party may cancel this Contract with the deposit returned to the Purchaser.

FINANCING COSTS

The Purchaser will often ask the Seller to pay closing costs in addition to the Seller's normal costs The amount and nature of lender fees is limited only by the lending institution's creativity. Define the parties' responsibilities clearly.

Clause [55] fixes the Seller's contribution. Clause [58] fixes the rate and allows the points to float. Clause [59] could protect the Seller.

[55] Seller's Points Fixed

Loan Fees: based on the financing terms specified, the Purchaser shall pay up to the first $_____ of the total lender charges. The Seller shall pay the next $_____ of the lender charges and the Purchaser shall pay the remainder of the total charges. The Purchaser is to pay the initial mortgage insurance (if any), loan assumption fee (if any) and any other allowable charges made by lender.

For VA financing add [56], FHA add [57]

[56] VA Financing add to [55]

Purchaser shall pay any applicable VA funding fee and the Seller will pay all other lender charges which cannot, by regulation, be charged to the Purchaser.

[57] FHA financing add to [55]

The Seller will pay all other lender charges which cannot, by regulation, be charged to the Purchaser.

[58] Rate Fixed, Points to Float

Purchaser has agreed to accept a loan at the rate of _____% per annum and Seller agrees to pay the discount points required at settlement to obtain that rate. To limit points, add [59].

[59] Point Limit

The Seller shall not pay more than $_____ toward discount points plus normal loan fees and expenses or Seller may cancel this Contract with the deposit returned to Purchaser.

[60] Subsidy Provided by Seller

Note: This clause is not appropriate for subsidies handled by the lender.

In addition to discount points charged by the Lender, Seller will escrow for the Purchaser $_____ utilized at the rate of $_____ per month to subsidize the Purchaser's loan payments. The Seller shall receive any funds remaining if the loan is prepaid.

FINANCING, OWNER HELD

If the owner held financing is part of an assumption transaction, you may need a clause to adjust the loan amount or downpayment if the amount of the assumed loan changes. See Clauses [53] and [54].

[61] Note Terms

Purchaser shall give and Seller shall hold a Deferred Purchase Money Deed of Trust (or Mortgage) and negotiable Note secured on the property. The Note amount is $_____ due _____ years from date and bear interest at the rate of _____% per annum, payable in (monthly/semi-annual, quarterly) installments of $_____ commencing (30 days from the date of settlement/or the first of the month with interest for the first month prorated). Payments apply first to interest then to principal.

The Deed of Trust (or Mortgage) shall be a (first/second/third) lien on the property. The Deed of Trust (or Mortgage) shall require the maker provide the Noteholder with written receipts or other evidence of payment of real estate taxes and hazard insurance within ten (10) business days of their due date. The Noteholder shall be provided with the original insurance policy and renewals showing the Noteholder as loss payee for full replacement value of the amount of all loans. Failure to comply shall be a default.

If any monthly payment is thirty (30) days or more in arrears, or in the event of default under any senior deed of trust (mortgage), the Note shall be in default. In the event of default, the Noteholder may declare the entire balance due and payable and commence foreclosure proceedings. Any installment not received within ten (10) days of the due date shall incur a late charge of 5%.

Should the property securing the note be sold, transferred, conveyed or alienated in any way, except by death, the entire balance shall be due and payable at Noteholder's option unless expressly approved in writing by the Noteholder. An Attorney at Law selected by Seller shall prepare the loan documents.

The Note may be paid in full or in part at any time...
Option 1 - without penalty. or,
Option 2 - with a prepayment penalty of _____% of the principal prepaid. or,
Option 3 - without penalty after _____ years but with a penalty of _____%
of the principal prepaid before that time.

Note: Add [66] for a wrap around note.

[62] Seller Holding Loan - Contingency for Credit Report

This contract is contingent on Purchaser furnishing Seller (or the buyer of the Note) with an acceptable credit report and financial statement. Purchaser shall furnish this data within 5 business days and promptly comply with additional requests of Seller. Seller shall have 2 business days after delivery of all data to approve the credit in writing or cancel this contract with the deposit returned to Purchaser. Approval must not be withheld unreasonably.

[63] Contingency for the Sale of a Seller-Held Note

This contract is contingent until (date/time) on the Seller's obtaining a written commitment for the sale of the Seller-held Note at a discount not more than _____% of the principal balance. The Seller must notify the Purchaser or the Selling Agent in writing before the deadline to cancel this contract, with the deposit returned to the Purchaser, otherwise, this Contract is in full force and effect.

[64] Deferred Interest

The payment as stated is not sufficient to repay interest charged on the Note and this deferred interest shall be...

Option 1 - added to principal and bear interest at the rate stated in the note. OR

Option 2 - deferred until maturity but shall not added to principal and shall not bear interest.

[65] Balloon Payment

This regular payments on this Note will not pay it in full. Approximately $_____ will be due at maturity. The Seller has not agreed to extend or refinance this payment. Neither the Seller nor the Agent has represented that mortgage money will be available from other sources to refinance this obligation.

FINANCING, WRAP AROUND LOANS

Wrap around loans are sometimes called "all-inclusive" because the note includes the balance of an existing note. Think of the noteholder as a lender who has, himself, borrowed the money loaned. As the Purchaser makes payments, the noteholder pays back his own loan.

Wrap around loans are useful when:

(a) there is favorable financing on the property but it contains a prepayment penalty, or
(b) the Seller wants to monitor the payments to be sure they are made, or
(c) where the Seller wants to protect his VA eligibility (see [47] - [50], or
(d) where the Seller wants to boost his yield to make up for a lower selling price. The holder of the wrap around is often able to make a profit on the existing financing, as the rate he charges can be more than the rate he pays.

The buyer benefits from a wrap because he doesn't need to meet the credit requirements of an institutional lender. Also, the interest rate he pays could be lower than the rate demanded by a lender who is not making a profit on the existing financing.

The Article in Section 3 of this Book explains the Contract for Deed method of using wrap around financing.

If the existing loan contains a prepayment penalty or negative amortization, be sure to reflect it in the wrap around or the noteholder will have a nasty surprise at the time of payoff.

[66] Basic Wrap Around Provision - Add to Clause [61] for a Seller-held Note.

This is a wrap around note and includes the balance of an existing loan for $_____ payable by Seller to _____. The wrap around note is conditioned on its holder assuming responsibility for forwarding the appropriate amount of any payment received from the Purchaser to the holder of the existing loan in accord with its amortization schedule. If either the Purchaser or the wrap around noteholder default in this obligation, the other may forward the necessary payments on his behalf.

[67] Optional Provisions

PREPAYMENT - Prepayments shall apply first to the balance owed the wrap around noteholder over the existing loan. When the Purchaser has paid that amount, in full, Purchaser may assume the existing loan and obtain a release of the wrap around note.

ESCROW AGENT - The Purchaser will make monthly payments to an independent escrow agent who will disburse to the existing noteholders and to the wrap around noteholder, at Purchaser's expense.

DUE ON SALE - This Deed of Trust (Mortgage) shall be subject to call or modification of its terms in the event of sale or conveyance of the property, notwithstanding any provisions contained in the existing Deed of Trust (Mortgage).

GIFT LETTER CONTINGENCY

Other clauses may put the Purchaser in default if he does not have the funds necessary to settle. See [40]. If the Purchaser contemplates a gift letter, he may need additional time and a contingency.

[68] Gift Letter Contingency

This Contract is contingent until (date) on the Purchaser's obtaining a gift letter, satisfactory to the lender, for $_____. If the Purchaser is unable to obtain the gift letter, he must invoke this contingency by delivering a written release and notice canceling the contract by the date specified or the contingency will be deemed satisfied. If the Purchaser cancels the Contract he will receive a refund of the deposit.

HOMEOWNER'S ASSOCIATION

Disclose any mandatory Condominium or Homeowner's Associations. These may require special disclosures or contingencies that vary from state to state. Check your state law for particular requirements or wording.

[69] Association Disclosure

Purchaser understands the property is subject to restrictive covenants that regulate the use of the property and require membership in a Homeowner's or Condominium Association. The mandatory payment to the association is $_____ per (month/quarter).

Seller warrants there are no special assessments against the property. OR

Seller discloses a special assessment of $_____ levied for (purpose). The Seller will pay $_____, at settlement and the Purchaser will pay the balance as required.

[70] Request for Association Disclosure (Note: This is a general clause and may not meet the requirements of the your state. Consult your state law for specific requirements.)

This property is in a development requiring membership in a homeowner's or condominium association.

Seller will provide, at Seller's/Purchaser's expense, a disclosure packet described below. If Seller does not provide the packet within ten days, Purchaser may declare the contract canceled or extend the period, in writing, from time to time.

The disclosure packet will contain, among other information: copy of the current declaration, articles of incorporation and by-laws, rules and regulations and architectural control guidelines, current budget and fiscal information, assessments for the property, whether or not there is an entity or facility to which the property owner may be liable for fees or charges, the amount of these charges, capital expenditures expected in the next two years, a summary of the reserve and replacement funds, information about pending law suits, insurance coverage, and notice of any architectural control or maintenance violations affecting the property.

This provision does not create a contingency on Purchaser's acceptance of the contents of the disclosure or any liability on the part of the Seller if the Association should fail to provide the requested information.   OR

This Contract is contingent on Purchaser's review and acceptance of the disclosure packet. This Contract may be canceled by Purchaser executing a written addendum, within three days following receipt of the disclosure packet, declining the disclosures and invoking this contingency.

INSPECTIONS, HOME

Smart buyers insist on a professional home inspection.

Listing agents may suggest an inspection done at the time of listing to uncover potential problems. This might also help deal with an unrealistic Seller. A reasonably clear report can be good advertising and avoid delays and kick-outs caused by a Purchaser adding his own inspection contingency.

The Agent has a duty of fairness to all parties and cannot conceal, or assist the seller in concealing a known defect.

Avoid the use of ambiguous terms such as "Satisfactory" in a contingency.

Give the Seller an option to make repairs, rather than allow the Purchaser to use little repairs as an excuse to cancel.

[71] Contingency For Home Inspection

The ALTERNATE clause changes the contingency to a "free look" for the buyer and he can cancel the contract without giving a reason or he can list specific repairs.

This contract is contingent until (time/date) upon inspection of the property by a home inspector at Purchaser's expense. The contingency will end at that time unless Purchaser delivers a contract addendum listing specific deficiencies for repair with a copy of the inspection report. ALTERNATE: The contingency will end at that time unless Purchaser delivers a contract addendum either cancelling the contract or requesting specific repairs.

The Seller may elect, within 3 Days of receipt, to remedy some or all of the items by responding to the Purchaser's addendum in writing.

If the Seller rejects the addendum or makes a counter-offer, the Purchaser shall have 3 Days to respond to the counter-offer or remove this contingency and take the property "as is."

If there is no written agreement within the times stated, this contract shall cancel with the deposit returned to the Purchaser.

The Seller's warranties about the condition of the property, appliances and systems are not altered by this contingency. The Seller must remedy any deficiencies in these items whether noted on the inspection or the pre-settlement walk through. Seller grants access to the property for an inspector of Purchaser's choice to conduct the inspection.

[72] Notice of Inspection Results and Demand

Purchaser delivers the attached Inspection Report in accord with the Home Inspection Contingency and removes the contingency provided Seller agrees to correct the following items before settlement:

(list specific deficiencies)

If the Seller does not complete all of the repairs before settlement, Seller agrees to escrow 150% of their estimated cost and complete them within 15 days after settlement or Purchaser may use the escrowed funds to complete the repairs.

Note: The seller may elect to sign the notice and demand, counter-offer or reject the demand. But, if the defect is covered by another warranty in the contract the seller must make the repair.

INSPECTION, RADON

[73] Radon Inspection Contingency

This contract is contingent until (time/date) on Purchaser's obtaining a radon screening measurement and report, at Purchaser's expense. The Seller shall grant the testing company access to the Property and maintain "closed-house" conditions, as recommended by the testing company.

The contingency will end at that time unless Purchaser delivers a copy of the report with a contract addendum stating that radon was found at levels exceeding U.S. Environmental Protection Agency action levels and that the Purchaser finds these levels unacceptable. The Seller may elect, within 5 Days of receipt, whether or not he will attempt to correct the condition.

If the Seller agrees to take remedial action to achieve the required screening measurement, Seller will furnish and pay for another inspection report demonstrating the condition remedied prior to settlement. If the Seller elects not to correct the condition, or if later inspections continue to show unacceptable elevated levels, Purchaser shall have 3 Days to remove this contingency and accept the radon condition or this Contract is canceled with the deposit returned to the Purchaser.

This clause does not create a warranty and if continuing inspections show the condition remains, the Purchaser's sole remedy shall be to cancel this contract.

[74] Notice of Inspection Results and Demand

Purchaser delivers the attached Inspection Report in accord with the Radon Inspection Contingency. The levels of radon are not acceptable to the Purchaser.

Seller agrees to take remedial action, before settlement, at Seller's expense as follows:

(list specific remedial action)

Seller will furnish and pay for another inspection report demonstrating the condition remedied prior to settlement.

This clause does not create a warranty and if continuing inspections show the condition remains, the Purchaser's sole remedy shall be to cancel this contract.

Note: The seller may elect to sign the notice and demand, counter-offer or reject the demand.

INSPECTION, TERMITE

What area does the contract cover? Treating a wood pile at the back of the lot can be very costly and unnecessary.

Does the Seller repair prior damage, even if there is no active infestation? FHA & VA will require such repairs.

Suggest ordering the inspection at time of listing to avoid later surprises, especially if the house has not been inspected regularly or is not under warranty.

Be sure the inspector knows if you are dealing with a VA or FHA loan as they require a special inspection form.

Check to see if the company will issue a warranty to the Purchaser. Ask if it covers damage repair or treatment only.

[75] Termite Inspection (Seller to Repair)

Seller will furnish, at settlement, a report (and warranty?) from a licensed pest control firm. The report must show the house and any other dwelling or attached structures or garages within the property lines free of visible termite or other wood destroying insect infestation, structural or visible damage. The inspection can be no more than 30 days before settlement.

If the report fails to meet these criteria, Seller is to take immediate steps to exterminate any infestations and repair damage before settlement. If these can not be accomplished before settlement, the Seller will escrow funds equal to 150% of the estimated cost to guarantee completion.

The (Selling or Listing) Agent is authorized to order the necessary inspection.

Limit on Costs: See [86] & [87].

INSPECTION, WELL AND SEPTIC

Be very careful that you represent the property accurately. If you mistakenly list and sell the property as having public sewer or water, and it doesn't, you may end up paying for the hookup.

Septic fields must be in active use at least 30 days before inspection. Many wells fail the first inspection. Be sure to order inspections in advance or prepare the Seller for escrows.

Check number of bedrooms and appliances against the septic permit.

Spell out well and septic requirements in the contract as not all jurisdictions require an inspection although VA/FHA or the lender may have requirements.

VA or lender may require hookup to public system if available.
VA/FHA may also require lead testing in addition to bacteriological.

[76] Warranty and Inspections

Seller warrants that septic and well systems, including pumps and all equipment, will be in good working order at settlement. Seller will furnish Purchaser with a certificate from the appropriate governmental authority, or private company, indicating the water supply meets construction and design standards and is acceptable based on the results of bacteriological tests.

Seller will furnish Purchaser with a certificate from the appropriate governmental authority, or private company, indicating the septic system is functioning properly and meets design and capacity requirements. These inspections can be made no more than 30 days before settlement.

[77] Repairs

If either system is substandard or requires repair, Seller will repair before settlement and furnish evidence of the repair and another inspection demonstrating the deficiency remedied. If Seller does not complete the repairs and reinspection before closing, Purchaser may elect to close and Seller will escrow funds equal to 150% of the anticipated repair costs.

LEASE TRANSFER

The Seller usually delivers possession at settlement, but with investment property the lease may transfer to the Purchaser. If the lease does not transfer, be sure

Seller can get tenant out in time for settlement. A month to month lease requires notice before the first of month to terminate at the end of that month.

If the lease transfers, you must be certain tenant has no defenses to payment of rent. An "estoppel certificate" is a statement from the tenant affirming the lease and agreeing to pay the rent.

[78] Lease Transfer

Seller will transfer to Purchaser, at settlement, the attached lease together with a security deposit of $_____. The parties will pro-rate the rent to the date of settlement. Seller warrants the lease is bona fide; rent will be current; the tenant has no defenses to the payment of rent; and there have been no modifications of the lease not disclosed in this contract. Seller will deliver to Purchaser, at settlement, an estoppel certificate from tenant certifying Seller's warranties are true.

NEW HOME CONTINGENCY

If the Seller needs time to find his house of choice, he may want the sale contract contingent until he does.

[79] Contingent on Seller Purchasing Home of Choice

This Contract is contingent until (date/time) on the Seller purchasing a home of his choice. This contingency will expire and the Contract be in full force and effect unless Seller delivers notice before the deadline declaring the Contract canceled with the deposit refunded to the Purchaser.

OCCUPANCY AGREEMENTS

At a minimum, the agreement should address: Security deposit, term, rent amount, condo or homeowner fees, penalty rent if property is not vacated on the end of term, responsibility for utilities and repairs, pre-occupancy walk through inspection and insurance. If you know the parties will need an occupancy agreement, deal with it as part of the contract. The easiest way to do this is to attach the occupancy agreement to the contract as an addendum.

Never let a Purchaser use the property, even to store furniture, without a written agreement from the Seller.

WARNING: On vacant properties or properties occupied or used by others, the owner should have in force a Fire and Extended Coverage Insurance Policy and an Owners Landlord and Tenant Liability Policy, not a Homeowner's Policy. These coverages protect the Owner and afford no protection to the Occupant. The Occupants should consult their own insurance agent for coverage of their belongings and liability.

[80] Occupancy Addendum

The parties have executed the Occupancy Agreement attached to this contract as an Addendum. The dates of occupancy and total rental amounts are subject to adjustment by mutual agreement but in no event...

Option 1 - may Purchaser occupy before (date).

Option 2 - may Seller occupy beyond (date).

[81] Purchaser's Pre-Settlement Occupancy Agreement

This Agreement is made on _____ 20____ as part of a Sales Contract dated _____, 20____ between:

_____ (Purchaser) and
_____ (Seller) for the following Property:

_____.

In consideration of the mutual terms of this Agreement, the Seller grants and the Purchaser accepts occupancy of the Property before settlement on the following terms and conditions:

1. Deposit   Purchaser deposits with (Selling Company, Listing Company or Seller) $_____ ("Additional Deposit") by cashier's or certified check. The Additional Deposit is held, first as security for this Agreement and if funds remain after satisfying these obligations, as an additional deposit under the Sales Contract.

2. Occupancy Charge   Purchaser will pay the Seller $_____ for the period between the date of occupancy, _____, and the estimated date of settlement, _____. Purchaser will pay the occupancy charge , in advance, at the rate of $_____ per (month or day). This amount will adjust on a pro rata basis to the actual date of settlement or Purchasers' vacating the Property. Only the unused part of the occupancy charge is a credit toward the purchase price. The parties agree the occupancy charge is not rent, and this Agreement is not a lease, but a temporary right of use and is not subject to Landlord Tenant law. This temporary right of use is exclusively for _____ number of occupants and the following pets: _____

3. Equipment Condition and Maintenance   Purchaser will inspect the Property before occupancy. Purchaser accepts full responsibility for maintenance and repair of the Property, including all appliances, equipment and landscaping at occupancy except for defects noted in writing delivered to the Seller. Occupancy, without written objection to defects, satisfies the warranty provisions of the Sales Contract. The warranty provisions and representations in the Sales Contract will govern any exceptions noted.

4. All Contingencies Removed   Purchaser warrants he has the ability to settle in accord with the contract. Purchaser's occupancy satisfies and removes any contingencies in the Sales Contract, with the exception of:_____.

5. Alterations and Risk of Loss The Purchaser will not detract from or devaluate the marketability or value of the Property. The Purchaser will not alter the Property without written approval of the Seller. The Purchaser accepts responsibility for any redecorating costs, material and labor incurred in advance of final settlement. Purchaser's personal Property, placed on the premises, shall be at his own risk. The risk of loss or damage to the Property by fire, act of God, or other casualty passes to the Purchaser at occupancy. The Purchaser shall hold Seller harmless from loss or damage to any personal property or bodily injury to any persons. The Purchaser will place insurance covering the structure, personal property, and liability prior to occupancy.

Seller is advised to consult with his own insurance agent regarding coverage.

Seller and Seller's agents shall have access to the Property at reasonable times and on reasonable notice for inspections and emergencies.

6. Utilities   Purchaser will transfer and pay all utilities as of the date of occupancy.

7. Failure to Close and Default   If the sale does not close, per the Sales Contract, except for Seller's default, or if the Purchaser is in default of the Contract, the Purchaser will vacate in a peaceable manner within five days of notice. Purchaser will immediately permit the Seller to place a lock box on the Property for access and permit showing the Property during reasonable hours. Purchaser must surrender the premises in the same condition as granted, properly maintained and cleaned, and return all keys.

In the case of Seller's default, the Purchaser has the option, without prejudicing any other legal rights, to continue to occupy the Property at the stated occupancy charge or may vacate the Property and receive a return of any remaining Additional Deposit.

The Purchaser authorizes the deduction from the Additional Deposit of any unpaid occupancy charges and costs to restore the premises to its condition at the time of Purchaser's pre-occupancy. If the Purchaser does not vacate, as requested, the periodic rate specified above will double on a daily basis. The Purchaser authorizes the Seller to also deduct those amounts. If these are insufficient, Purchaser will pay the difference immediately upon demand. The Purchaser will also be liable for the costs of enforcing this Agreement.

8. Other Terms: _____

add signature lines for all parties

[82] Seller's Continued Occupancy Agreement

This Agreement is made on _____ 20____ as part of a Sales Contract dated_____, 20____ between:

_____ (Purchaser) and

_____ (Seller) for the following Property:

_____.

In consideration of the mutual terms of this Agreement, Purchaser permits Seller to occupy the Property after the time of settlement on the following terms and conditions:

1. Occupancy Charge   Seller will pay the Purchaser, at settlement, an occupancy charge for the interim period between the estimated date of settlement, _____ and _____. The actual amount of the occupancy charge will be the sum of the principal, interest taxes, insurance and homeowner or condominium fee paid by Purchaser and is estimated to be $_____ per month for a total of $_____. If the occupancy period is more than on month, the Seller will pay monthly, in advance. This amount will adjust on a pro rata basis to the actual date the Seller vacates the Property. Purchaser will refund any unused part of the occupancy charge. The parties agree the occupancy charge is not rent and this Agreement is not a lease, but a temporary right of use and is not subject to Landlord Tenant law.

2. Absolute Deadline   Seller must vacate and tender possession of the Property and keys to Purchaser on or before midnight, _____.

3. Security Deposit   Seller will escrow, at settlement $_____ as a security deposit to be held by:_____ ("Escrow Agent"). The Purchaser may, without prejudicing other legal rights and remedies, use all or any part of the deposit to defray costs incurred because of the Seller's breach of this Agreement. Purchaser will conduct a post occupancy inspection of the Property within 5 days of written notice Seller has vacated and Deliver to Seller and Escrow Agent a list of deficiencies within 3 days thereafter. If the Escrow Agent does not receive this notice, the Escrow Agent may release funds to the Seller and be held harmless by the parties. If notice is delivered, the Seller will receive the remaining security deposit after correcting any deficiencies.

4. Maintenance   Seller will maintain and deliver the Property including all equipment, appliances and landscaping in keeping with the provisions of the Sales Contract.

5. Utilities   Seller will keep all utilities registered in Seller's name and pay the costs until vacating the premises.

6. Risk of Loss   Any personal property, not included in the sale, kept on the premises shall be at Seller's risk. Seller shall hold Purchaser harmless from loss or damage to any personal property or bodily injury to any persons having access to the Property.

Seller and Purchaser are advised to consult with their own insurance agents regarding coverage.

7. Access   Seller will permit Purchaser reasonable access to the Property and will deliver a key to Purchaser, at settlement. Seller will permit the Purchaser to place a lock box on the Property for access and permit showing the Property during reasonable hours 30 days before termination.

8. Default   The daily occupancy rate shall double if Seller fails to vacate the Property by the Absolute Deadline. Seller shall also be responsible for any expense incurred by Purchaser as a result of Seller's failure to vacate, such as, but not limited to temporary accommodations, furniture storage, added moving costs, and the costs of enforcing this Agreement.

9. Other Terms:_____ _____

add signature lines for all parties

OPTIONS

An option is an open offer until the expiration of a certain time or other conditions. An option is different than a right of first refusal. A right of first refusal is the right to match somebody else's offer. With a right of first refusal, you do not know the terms in advance. An option contains a complete understanding of the terms when written.

The person having the option must give some consideration for it. This could be a non-refundable fee. In a lease with option to buy, the consideration could be the rental of the property. If the option is exercised, the fee or part of the rent may or may not apply to the purchase price. The option should be definite in its term so there is no question when it expires.

Negotiate and execute a full sales contract so there is a complete agreement on the sale terms. The contract should contain a clause stating that it is the subject of an option and does not become effective until exercise of the option. Any reference to times for performance will not start to run until exercise.

[83] Option

In consideration of the payment of a non-refundable fee of $_____, Seller grants Purchaser the option to purchase the Property described in the attached Contract of Sale under all the terms and conditions found in that Contract.

If not exercised, this Option shall automatically expire (date or upon the happening of some event but no later than a certain date). Exercise shall be by delivering written notice to (Agent or Seller) and by the delivery of an additional deposit of $_____. The non-refundable fee (shall or shall not) be a credit toward the purchase price.

The effective date of the Contract shall be the date of delivery of the notice and all time periods set forth in the contract shall begin to run on that date.

[84] Lease - Purchase Option

First, agree on and execute a standard form lease and a contract. Then add the following as an additional provision to the lease. Add [85] to the contract. Commission terms should also be in the Contract.

In consideration of full performance of Tenant's obligations under this Lease, Seller grants to Purchaser the option to purchase the property described in the attached Contract of Sale under all the terms and conditions found in that

Contract. This option shall automatically terminate if Purchaser defaults under the Lease and the default remains uncured after five days written notice delivered to the Property.

This Option automatically expires (date or upon the happening of some event but no later than a certain date). Exercise shall be by delivering written notice to (Agent or Seller) and by the delivery of an additional deposit of $_____ .

OPTIONAL: $_____ from each monthly rental payment shall be an additional deposit and a credit toward the sale price.

The effective date of the Contract shall be the date of delivery of the notice and all time periods set forth in the contract shall begin to run on that date.

[85] Option Clause for Contract

This Contract is the subject of an Option Agreement and does not come into full force and effect until exercise of the Option. All effective dates in this Contract shall begin on the date of delivery of notice to (Agent or Seller).

REPAIRS

A more detailed discussion of "expected" repairs is in the sections on Home Inspections and Equipment and Property Condition.

A lender's appraisal or VA/FHA regulations may require repairs outside the original contemplation of the parties. The Contract should have a provision to deal with these situations.

[86] Repair Costs (Agreed Amount)

Seller will make any repairs required by the Lender, VA or FHA as a condition of providing the financing in this Contract. Provided, Seller's liability shall not exceed $_____ or Seller shall have the option to cancel this Contract with the deposit refunded to the Purchaser. The Seller must exercise this option within 5 Days of receiving written notice of the required repairs or this Contract will be in full force and effect.

This provision (does or does not) apply to Seller's responsibilities under other provisions of this Contract governing termite, well or septic inspections and requirements that appliances, heating and cooling equipment, electrical and plumbing systems be in working order at the time of settlement.

[87] Repair Costs (No Agreed Amount)

The Purchaser will notify the Seller immediately if the Lender, VA or FHA requires repairs to the property as a condition of providing the financing in this Contract. Purchaser must deliver a contract addendum listing specific deficiencies for repair with a copy of the lender's requirements. The Seller may elect, within 3 Days of receipt, to remedy some or all of the items by responding to the Purchaser's addendum in writing.

If the Seller rejects the addendum or makes a counter-offer, the Purchaser shall have 3 Days to respond to the counter-offer or take the property "as is" and accept responsibility for the remaining repairs.

If there is no written agreement within the times stated, this contract cancels with the deposit returned to the Purchaser.

This provision (does or does not) apply to Seller's responsibilities under other provisions of this Contract governing termite, well or septic inspections and requirements that appliances, heating and cooling equipment, electrical and plumbing systems be in working order at the time of settlement.

SETTLEMENT DATE

Most Contracts provide a specific settlement date or a "not later than" date. Many add an extension period for delays in obtaining financing, title reports or to clear minor title defects. Clause [88] is a clear cut-off with a return of the deposit. It does not require finding one party in default of the contract.

[88] Date

Provided the Seller is not the cause of delay, if settlement has not occurred by (date), Seller shall have the option to cancel this Contract or extend the time for settlement from time to time. If the Seller is the cause of delay, the Purchaser shall have the option to cancel the Contract or extend settlement from time to time.

If either party cancels the Contract, the deposit shall be returned to Purchaser.

STUDY CONTINGENCY

A study period allows the purchaser additional time to satisfy himself the property is suitable for his needs. The purchaser is usually allowed a great deal of discretion, and will use the word "satisfactory.". Commercial contracts often contain study contingencies.

[89] Study Contingency

This contract is contingent on the Purchaser obtaining satisfactory test results from engineering, boring, hazardous waste and soil studies and such other engineering, economic or general feasibility studies as Purchaser may desire. If, in Purchaser's sole discretion, Purchaser determines his development or use of the property is not feasible, he may cancel this Contract with the deposit refunded.

This Contract will be in full force and effect unless Purchaser delivers written notice of cancellation with a release by (date/time).

Seller grants access to the property to perform tests, surveys and studies so long as the studies do not change the present character or topography of the property. Purchaser shall repair all damage and hold the Seller harmless from any costs, claim actions or demands as a result of the tests.

SURVEYS

Surveys often reveal encroachments and errors in the legal description. Even when dealing with large acreage, the exact dimensions or boundaries are important.

Title insurance policies may not insure against survey matters unless the title company reviews a recent survey. Most lenders will not allow this exception in their title policy.

Often a survey that was done ten or twenty years ago will not agree with a survey done today, using more modern and accurate surveying instruments.

[90] Quantity of Land

The parties agree a boundary survey at the expense of (Purchaser and/or Seller?) will establish the exact dimensions and quantity of land conveyed. If the acreage varies from that set forth in the Seller's legal description, the price shall adjust at the rate of $_____ per acre. Provided, if the adjustment is more than ____% of the sales price, the party adversely affected may declare this contract canceled with the deposit returned to the Purchaser.

Any other discrepancy in the legal description must be insurable by a recognized title insurance company at regular rates or the Purchaser shall have the option to cancel this Contract with the deposit refunded.

[91] Easements and Encroachments

The Seller grants the Purchaser access to the property to obtain a boundary survey and to locate any easements or encroachments that may affect the intended use of the property. The Purchaser will report any objectionable matters to the Seller in writing by (date). The Seller shall have ten days to resolve the objections. If the Seller can not resolve the objections within that time, the Purchaser shall have the option to cancel the Contract receive a refund of the deposit.

TAX DEFERRED EXCHANGES

Section Three contains an article on tax deferred exchanges.

[92] Tax Deferred Exchange Listing

The owner intends to accomplish a tax deferred exchange. Any contract should provide for Purchaser cooperation. Contact lister for details.

[93] Tax Deferred Exchange Sales Contract

This transaction will be a Section 1031 Tax Deferred Exchange at no additional expense or liability to the Purchaser. The intention of the Parties is for the Seller/Exchanger to use Section 1031 of the Internal Revenue Code to postpone taxes by exchanging this Property for other property (insert description or "to be designated later and acquired through a trust established at settlement"). The Purchaser and Seller/Exchanger will execute necessary documents to complete the exchange, including any assignments or trust agreements.

The Seller will pay all expenses associated with the tax deferred exchange and hold the Purchaser harmless from any liability in connection therewith.

All references to "Seller" in the Contract shall mean Seller/Exchanger.

[94] Tax Deferred Exchange Purchase Contract

This transaction will be a Section 1031 Tax Deferred Exchange at no additional expense or liability to the Seller. The intention of the parties is for the Purchaser/Exchanger to use Section 1031 of the Internal Revenue Code to postpone taxes by receiving this Property through an exchange for (insert description of property the Purchaser/Exchanger sold) or the escrowed proceeds from that sale/exchange. The parties will cooperate and execute necessary documents to complete the exchange.

The Purchaser will pay all expenses associated with the tax deferred exchange and hold the Seller harmless from any liability in connection therewith.

All references to "Purchaser" in the Contract shall mean Purchaser/Exchanger.

POWERS OF ATTORNEY

A power of attorney is an important legal document. In many states a non-lawyer cannot prepare one. Even filling out a simple form is usually prohibited. There are special requirements for powers of attorney and many of the forms in common use may not be sufficient for your particular transaction. Always check with the settlement attorney and the lender if there is any chance a power of attorney may be involved.

Signing documents on behalf of another party invites considerable liability. Be sure you have explained everything and keep notes of your conversation. Fax or email the document whenever possible and get a signature back.

Be mindful of agency responsibilities. A selling sub-agent represents the seller and can not act as power of attorney for the buyer. A Buyer Agent could act as power of attorney for the buyer.

The best method is to fax or email the written document for original signatures, or use an overnight delivery service such as Federal Express.

Sometimes you can email a document but the party at the other end has no way to scan and return it. The following clauses are designed if you are going to use an email as confirmation, rather than a scan or fax of the entire document.

[95] Acceptance of Offer or Counter offer

We accept the (purchaser's name) offer to purchase our property at

_____.

OR

We counter the (purchaser's name) offer to purchase our property at
_____ as follows:

List those items to be changed. We accept all other terms and conditions of the contract.

[96] Contract Amendment

We accept the amendment to Paragraph _____ of the purchase agreement dated _____ on (address) to add the following clause: (insert clauses) All other terms of this contract shall remain in full force and effect.

[97] Occupancy Agreement Authorization

We accept the Occupancy Agreement for (name) on our property at (address) at
$_____ per day starting on (date). Purchaser agrees at time of

occupancy to deposit an additional $_____ with (agent). Settlement on or before (date). (We are aware written loan commitment has not been received.)

[98] Signature Line for Contract

Acceptance on behalf of _____ per authority contained in email dated _____.

BY: _____

[99] Listing Agreement

In consideration of your efforts expended and your agreement to list our home in any Multiple Listing Service, we grant you the exclusive right to sell our home at (address). (Specific terms, sales price, settlement, VA, chattels, compensation, any contingencies).

[100] Offer to Purchase

We offer the owners of (address) to purchase that property as follows:

Sales price $_____, Cash down payment $_____. We will place/assume a first trust (conv./VA/FHA/etc.) of $_____ at _____% interest for _____ years $_____ PI. Second trust to be held by seller of $_____ per month due in full in _____ years. Settlement to occur on or before (date). Chattels to include _____.
Earnest money deposit of $_____ by (check, note due on _____ follows immediately).

If applicable add: Subject to VA/FHA appraisal of no less than $_____.

(Company name) standard form contract to be used for this transaction.

Any contingencies.
Any addendums.

[101] Authority of Wife/Husband to Sign

I authorize (name) as my agent to sign my name to any and all contracts of sale and other necessary documents pertaining to the purchase/sale of (address) for $_____. The affixing of my signature by my agent to any such documents shall bind me to all terms therein.

The non-veteran spouse may not sign for the veteran spouse without a Power of Attorney in VA cases. VA requires special power of attorney language. Use the following language.

[102] Kick Out Clause

This Contract shall cancel with the Purchaser's deposit fully returned if the (Seller or Purchaser) does not sign this Contract by (date, time).

SECTION THREE - ARTICLES

AGENCY

VIRGINIA'S BROKERAGE WITHOUT AGENCY – ILLUSTRATING THE DIFFERENCE BETWEEN TRADITIONAL AGENCY AND MODERN REPRESENTATION

Effective October 1, 1995, Virginia real estate licensees entered a new status - free from the unreasonable and contradictory bonds of common law agency. Virginia's new agency law specifically abrogated the common law of agency and implied fiduciary duties. In its place, the law defines a "brokerage relationship" and sets out the parameters for the new "standard agency" Representation.

This landmark legislation paved the way for effective dual representation and eliminated the implied fiduciary duties that have long plagued real estate licensees. The law does not turn real estate licensees into facilitators, counselors or some other hybrid. Instead, it defines the exact relationship and duties a real estate licensee owes to clients and customers, without resorting to vague or contradictory fiduciary standards.

First, some background on the law of agency: A true agent is one who has power to bind the person he represents (called the "principal"). An example would be a trustee, or executor of a last will and testament. With the power to bind the principal comes a duty to zealously and unselfishly represent and defend that principal, to the exclusion of all others, including yourself. Those duties sound like the Boy Scout Code: trustworthy, loyal, helpful, friendly, courteous, kind, obedient, cheerful, thrifty, brave, clean and reverent. A real estate agent is not a true agent with power to bind either the buyer or seller. However, a long line court decisions, held the real estate agent to the fiduciary duties without the powers.

To make matters worse, an agency relationship may be implied. No writing is necessary. It can arise from a party's actions, not his words. You can be an unintentional agent if someone has come to rely upon you.

Common law fiduciary duties are what gave real estate agents problems with dual agency representation. Common law agency principles would suggest one party cannot zealously represent two different and opposing sides of the transaction unless the two parties agree to the dual representation. Thus, the distinction between disclosed and undisclosed dual agency.

Undisclosed dual agency was and still will be treated as fraud. Fraud in the transaction means one of the parties may rescind (cancel). The buyer sues the agent for fraud and the seller sues the agent because the transaction failed. The agent is liable for damages from both parties and may lose a license as well.

Even in cases of disclosed dual agency, Courts have struggled with the concept of representing more than one party in the transaction. The very idea flies in the face of common law agency principles. What degree of disclosure is adequate? Did the parties really understand the implications? Any doubt will most likely be resolved against the licensed professional whose duty it was to protect the client.

Agents following their common law fiduciary duties found other conflicts as well. State regulatory boards seek to protect the public by calling for full disclosure. Such disclosure might not be in the client's best interest. Therefore, the agent might be required to disclose information while a Court would find that disclosure a breach of duty to the client. There are similar conflicts between the REALTOR Code of Ethics and the common law.

This article summarizes the Virginia law and compares it with prior practice. Realizing it is a bit odd to call a fifteen year-old law "new," we'll still use the term to distinguish it from the "old law" which refers to the common statutory and case law of agency with implied fiduciary duties. Capitalized words are defined in the new law.

First, a comparison:

Fiduciary Responsibilities

The old law required adherence to abroad range of implied fiduciary obligations leading to conflicting court decisions and responsibilities.

The new law specifically abrogated common law agency and fiduciary responsibility in brokerage relationships and replaced them with specific duties as outlined below. Those are an agent's only duties unless a written contract establishing the brokerage relationship calls for more.

Disclosure of Brokerage Relationships

Old law required verbal and written disclosure of the agent's representation without specifying a format.

The new law only required agency disclosure to persons who are not Clients. You do not need to give an agency disclosure form to someone if you have a written agreement to represent them. Such a disclosure would be redundant.

The new law provided "safe harbor" forms for both single agency, dual agency and designated representative dual agency.

Timing for the disclosure is the same as before. Verbal disclosure is made "upon having substantive discussions about a specific property or properties." Written disclosure can follow "at the earliest practical time" but not later than the "time when specific real estate assistance is first provided."

You only need to keep the agency disclosure forms for fully executed contracts, not all offers. You must keep them for three years.

For lease transactions, disclosure can be in the application or lease, whichever first occurs.

Disclosure of Property Condition

The old Real Estate Board regulation said the agent must disclose all material information related to the property "reasonably available to the licensee." This meant agents had a duty to inquire and disclose everything they should have found. The standard was what you should have known, not what you knew. Because, it included all material information related to the property, it could be interpreted to include deaths and other stigmatizing factors.

The new law says licensees must treat customers honestly and not knowingly give them false information. You are expected to disclose what you actually know, not what you could have discovered. The disclosure is limited to the physical condition of the property.

Vicarious Liability

Under the old law an agent could be held liable for passing along false information received from a client. The client could be liable for negligent actions by the licensee and sub-agents.

Under the new law, agents may rely on what they are told unless they have knowledge the information is false or act in reckless disregard of the truth. No knowledge or information is imputed among the agents, brokers or clients. There is no longer vicarious liability for the actions or statements of others unless you know of a misrepresentation and you don't take reasonable steps to correct it.

Dual Agency

You become an agent by entering into an agency agreement to represent someone or by acting in such a way that they come to rely on you as their agent. Dual agency occurs when one agent or company represents both sides of the transaction.

The old law allowed disclosed dual agency (jokingly known as "duel" agency) but left many agents, buyers and sellers uncomfortable. It was not clear if one licensee could act as a dual agent for both a buyer and seller although practice suggested one company could perform both roles. Since there was no officially approved form of disclosure, companies and REALTOR associations designed their own in the hope it would meet with court approval, if tested.

The new law specifically allows one agent to represent both the buyer and the seller. Disclosed dual agency is possible because the agent no longer owes a fiduciary duty to represent one party exclusively. However, the agent must keep confidential personal and financial information and any other information the Client requests remain confidential.

The new law also introduced a new concept called the "Designated Representative." If the buyer and seller are not comfortable with one agent representing them both, or if two agents from the same company end up on different sides of the transaction, the broker may assign each party an agent to act as a Designated Representative. Neither agent is considered a dual agent although the broker is acting as a dual agent.

Revisions to the Listing Agreement and Buyer Agency Agreement discuss the future possibility of dual agency and ask the Client to consent in advance to disclosed dual agency or Designated Representation.

Agency Disclosure Forms

The law provides "safe harbor" disclosure forms for single agency, disclosed dual agency and designated representatives.

A single agent represents only one side of the transaction. If you are the lister and an unrepresented buyer appears at an open house, you should disclose you are representing the seller. You are not a dual agent. The single agency disclosure form contains a simple statement identifying your representation.

As a dual agent, you represent both sides of the transaction. The form states you represent more than one party. The parties are told you may not disclose to either of them information given to you in confidence unless the law requires you to. For example, you must still disclose material facts pertaining to the physical condition of the property or concerning the transaction which are actually known by you.

If the brokerage firm is representing both sides of the transaction, using two different agents, they act as Designated Representatives. The broker identifies the licensee/sales associate to act for each of the parties. The confidentiality requirements are the same provided the agent may disclose confidential information to the broker. However, the broker may not disclose confidential information to the other agent.

Withdrawal of Representation

Under the old law, it was not clear how an agent could withdraw if a dual agency situation arose and the client refused to consent. This could occur if the buyer, in a buyer agency relationship, decided to buy one of the agent's listings. A strict reading of fiduciary responsibilities would indicate the agent was obligated to continue to represent one party exclusively and could not quit.

The new law says you can withdraw, without penalty, and continue to represent one side to the transaction but you must maintain confidential that which was confidential. Hopefully this need will not arise, because the new Listing Agreement and Buyer Agency Agreement warns the parties of the possibility of dual representation and asks for their advance consent.

Ministerial Acts

Under the old law an agent who was too helpful to the other party might be accused of becoming an undisclosed dual agent. Since that amounted to fraud, the entire transaction would be in jeopardy and the agent liable for substantial damages.

The new law specifically allows one to perform "Ministerial Acts" for the other party without becoming their agent. Ministerial Acts are routine acts that do not require discretion or judgment by the licensee. Examples might be meeting the termite inspector or appraiser, or picking up and delivering papers. For an example of a non-ministerial act, consider the following: An agent representing the seller might recommend several home inspectors but would not want to select one for the buyer as that involves discretion and judgment.

What is the Same?

The new law still requires an agent to obey all applicable fair housing laws.

Disclosure of agency must be made as before. Verbal: upon having substantive discussions about a specific property and written: at the earliest practical time but not later than when specific real estate assistance is first provided.

The new law also still allows a brokerage relationship to come about through the actions of the parties. This leads to the dangerous paradox of being liable as an agent because someone thought you were their agent but not being able to collect a commission because your agreement was not in writing. You must always guard against the possibility of being considered an undisclosed dual agent. Don't let customers (as opposed to clients) rely upon you and your expertise.

Summary of Agent's Duties:

The Virginia law (Section 55.1-2130 – 2145) defines twelve basic duties expected of all agents. These duties may be expanded by a written agreement defining the brokerage relationship such as a listing or buyer agency agreement.

All Licensees whether representing buyers, sellers, tenants or landlords shall:

1. Disclose their Brokerage Relationships to persons who are not their Clients and disclose, to all parties, any changes in their relationship.

2. Perform according to the terms of their Brokerage Relationship. A Brokerage Relationship is a contractual relationship between a Client and a real estate licensee, engaged by the Client, to procure a ready, willing and able seller, buyer, option, tenant or landlord.

3. Seek a property, sale or lease at a price and with terms acceptable to the Client. However, the licensee is not obligated to seek other properties or offers to purchase or lease while the property or Client is subject to a contract of sale or lease, unless agreed to as part of the Brokerage Relationship or otherwise provided.

4. Present in a timely manner all written offers or counteroffers to and from the Client, even when the property or Client is already a party to another contract or lease.

5. Disclose to your Client all material facts related to the property or concerning the transaction of which you have actual knowledge. Compare this to the more limited obligation to disclose to a Customer (a party you do not represent) all material facts related to the physical condition of the property of which you have actual knowledge. You do not need to disclose other material facts to Customers. (Listing agents beware - the buyer agent is not obligated to tell you about the buyer's financial condition unless you ask as part of a counter-offer).

6. Account for, in a timely manner, all money and property received in which the Client has or may have an interest.

7. Maintain confidential all personal and financial information received from the Client and any other information that the client requests be maintained confidential unless otherwise provided by law or the Client consents in writing to the release of such information. You may reveal information required by law. The duty of confidentiality continues even after the transaction is over.

8. Exercise ordinary care. That is what a reasonable person would do as opposed to the more stringent "fiduciary" standard of care.

9. Comply with all provisions of Virginia law, all applicable fair housing statutes and regulations, and all other applicable statutes and regulations that are not in conflict with Virginia law.

10. A licensee engaged by a Client may, unless prohibited by law or the Brokerage Relationship may assist the other party or prospective other party by performing Ministerial Acts. Ministerial Acts do not violate the licensee's brokerage relationship with the Client unless expressly prohibited by the terms of the Brokerage Relationship. Ministerial Acts do not, by themselves, form a Brokerage Relationship with the Customer.

11. Treat all non-clients honestly and not knowingly give them false information.

12. A licensee engaged in a Brokerage Relationship with a Client does not breach any duty or obligation to the Client by showing properties in which the Client is interested to other prospective Clients or Customers, showing alternative properties to Customers or Clients, representing other Clients looking at the same or other properties, or by representing other parties who have properties for sale or lease.

In addition, Licensees engaged by an owner shall disclose to prospective buyers or tenants all material adverse facts pertaining to the physical condition of the property that are actually known by the licensee. A licensee shall not be liable for providing false information if the false information was provided to the licensee by another person and the licensee did not (i) have actual knowledge that the information was false or (ii) act in reckless disregard of the truth.

Why is the New Agency Law Good for Consumers and Licensees?

1. It clearly defines duties and responsibilities of licensees and eliminates confusing and conflicting court cases, laws and regulations.

2. It permits licensees to perform many ministerial acts without worrying about becoming unintended dual agents.

3. It eliminates vicarious liability a client may have had for the misrepresentations of his agent.

4. It requires the agent to maintain confidentiality even after the agency relationship has ended.

5. It lists exactly what customers and clients have a right to expect from their brokerage relationship unless that relationship is changed in writing.

BUYER AGENCY

In a traditional Multiple Listing System the listing agent represents the seller and extends a unilateral offer of sub-agency to other member of the system. In a sense, the listing agent is saying, "come work with me and I will share the commission with you." The key phrase is "work with me." In the past, that meant the selling agent was working for the listing agent and for the seller. It also meant the selling agent owed all the fiduciary duties described in the articles above and below to the seller and not to the buyer. Until very recently, it was virtually impossible for a buyer to have his own agent representing him exclusively. Heightened consumer awareness, sensitivity to the issues of dual agency, and a buyer's market all encourage the buyer agent concept.

Why would an agent want to be a Buyer Agent? Here's a summary of some reasons:

Many buyers take an agent's time for granted and show little loyalty. Agents don't want to waste their time with buyers who are not really serious. Agents know they will have undivided attention - especially if they ask for a retainer fee up front. Selling agents typically close only 10% of their buyers. Buyer agents claim to close 90-100% of their buyers. The buyer agent functions as a trusted and objective advisor, not a sales person.

A buyer agent can deal with property outside the MLS system. For example, a FSBO seller may not want to sign a listing with you but he will listen to your contract offer. A seller may be interested but not want to deal with the publicity and bother of a listing.

A buyer agent avoids dual agency traps. As a buyer agent, they represent only the buyer and don't face the problems of conflicting loyalty. They are not a sub-agent of the lister.

Why a Buyer Wants a Buyer Agent With buyer agency, also called buyer brokerage or single agency brokerage, each party has a professional representing his interests. The buyer gains access to the same services, skills and training formerly available only to sellers.

Buyer Agents are able to negotiate on behalf of the buyer. They can argue for the buyer's best interest. A Buyer Agent can take two contracts to a presentation and offer the lowest first. The Buyer Agent can hold power of attorney for the buyer and make changes to a contract or settle on the buyer's behalf. Sub-agents can't perform any of these functions.

Establishing a Fee   There are many variations of Buyer Agent fee arrangements. There are four choices: retainers, flat fees, hourly fees or percentage commissions. They can be combined. They buyer agent may ask for an up front retainer. This amount is usually $100 to $250 and serves two purposes. One, it eliminates buyers who are not serious. Second, it ties the buyer to the broker. After having spent money, he is not likely to buy from someone else. At a minimum the fee covers some of the agent's expenses. Sometimes, the fee is refunded at settlement.

Obviously the agent can't make a living on small retainers. The bulk of the compensation must come from settlement, hopefully paid by the seller. It is possible to be a buyer agent and have the seller pay the fee. A percentage commission, paid by the seller, is the most common arrangement. Percentage commissions tied to the selling price could be seen as a conflict of interest since they would lead the agent to show more expensive property. The buyer agents say this has not been a problem. Most folks buy the most home they can afford anyway. A flat fee based on the expected purchase price eliminates the conflict but may be hard to guess. Hourly fees make sense for general counseling but generally do not return enough to work for sales.

Usually, the buyer agent's fee is equal to the selling agent's portion of the commission as offered in the Multiple Listing System. It is paid by the seller out of the settlement. The seller's and the lister's net remains the same as with a conventional sub-agency sale.

Modern MLS systems provide the listing company will provide "cooperation and compensation" to a buyer agent although the amount of the compensation is not established by the organization that runs the MLS. The seller and the listing agent decide the buyer agent compensation. The listing agent then offers that compensation in the MLS and the National Association of REALTOR Code of the Ethics prohibits the buyer agent from attempting to renegotiate the offered commission. If the buyer agent doesn't like what is offered, he can show the buyer a different house. Depending on the number of buyers and buyer agents, sellers may have a hard time selling if they don't offer what is considered "full commission."

Whichever compensation method you choose, your agency agreement must be in writing.

See the Buyer Agent clauses in Section Two, [6] - [9].

DUAL AGENCY

Traditionally, a real estate agent has been the agent or representative of the Seller. This is a derivative of the listing agreement and, when the listing is a co-op, the unilateral offer of sub-agency made to other agents who produce a Purchaser ready willing and able to buy the property. Both the listing and selling agents represent the Seller unless the selling agent is working as a buyer agent pursuant to a written agreement with the Purchaser. Clause [6] contains a Buyer Agent Agreement.

It is a fundamental principal of agency that the agent is a fiduciary of the principal (Seller). The agent is in a position of trust requiring absolute loyalty, obedience, disclosure, confidence and diligence. The agent must disclose all facts learned about the Purchaser that may affect the Seller's decision This includes the Purchaser's admission that he will pay more for the property. The agent must exercise his best efforts to bring the Seller the highest price and best terms.

Dual agency, the representation of both sides in any transaction, places the agent in a position of conflicting loyalties. It is possible to become an unintentional dual agent without realizing it. The law regards the agent as representing both sides if that is what other people think he is doing. This is unintentional dual agency. Because it is unintentional, it is usually not disclosed. Intentional undisclosed dual agency is rare but the law does not distinguish between actual malicious fraud and unintentional or accidental lapses. All undisclosed dual agency is treated as FRAUD and risks strict legal consequences.

Undisclosed dual agency entitles either the Seller or Purchaser to void the transaction. They do not need to prove the dual agency damaged them. Any injured party may sue the agent for losses including those the Seller may suffer from losing the sale, attorney's fees, and punitive damages. The agent can forfeit the commission, even though the sale may go through. Fraud is a breach of public morals and may subject the agent to severe legal and professional censure.

The selling sub-agent may become an agent of the Purchaser without realizing it. You do not need compensation from the Purchaser or a written agreement. If the Purchaser is "counting on" the agent, or confides in the agent or related to the agent by blood, marriage or friendship, the law may make him a buyer agent. If the agent is also a cooperating sub-agent of the seller he has become a dual agent.

Some examples of unintentional dual agency by a selling sub-agent:

A selling sub-agent refers to the Purchaser as "my client" leading him to believe the agent is working for him.

Acting with a Power of Attorney for a Purchaser.

Purchasing one of your own or your company's listings.

Work with a family member or friend purchasing property.

You tell the Purchaser any of the following: "I'll negotiate the best price." "I'll take care of everything." "I'm sure the Seller will take less." "Don't bother with a house location survey (or home inspection etc.), I'm sure everything is OK." "You should use our company's title and escrow company to do the settlement."

A buyer agent would be able to handle all of the examples above without dual agency fears, as long as the seller and listing agent understood the buyer agent was not a selling sub-agent.

Clauses [3] or [4] disclose dual agency.

HOW TO HOLD TITLE

Suppose you are buying property with a friend, fiancé, relative or spouse. Did you know there are different types of joint ownership? Your choice has serious consequences; both on your estate, if you die, and on your rights while you live. There are three common types of joint ownership known as tenancies - all created in the deed giving you title. They are tenants in common, joint tenants and tenants by the entirety. These tenancies date their beginnings to medieval England and are best understood by examining the differences between them.

DISCLAIMER - This article is written for general information only. It is based on English Common Law and the law of Virginia. Community property states such as California and Texas have different rules. Laws vary from state to state. Be sure to check with a local real estate attorney for an interpretation of the law in your jurisdiction.

TENANTS IN COMMON   The law presumes tenants in common unless the deed you receive specifies otherwise. If one owner dies the property passes to his heirs, not necessarily the survivor. If there is a Will, it controls. Lacking a Will, state law provides rules for intestate succession. Persons who are not married or related usually use tenants in common.

A tenant in common may sell his interest without approval of the other owner. Unless specified otherwise, the law assumes you meant to have equal ownership.

TENANTS BY THE ENTIRETY   Tenancy by the entirety is only possible when the joint owners are husband and wife. Tenants by the entirety provides for a common law right of survivorship. The property goes automatically to the surviving spouse. No Will, probate or other legal action is necessary. One spouse can not use a Will to leave an interest to someone else.

This tenancy also follows the ancient legal theory that a married couple is one entity. Therefore, one owner may not convey an interest without the other. A creditor with a judgment against one of the owners cannot collect it from entirety property. If there is a judgment against one spouse, the settlement attorney will ask for a continuous marriage affidavit from the seller. In it, the sellers will certify they have been married for the entire time they owned the property. Then, the judgment does not attach to the property or the proceeds of sale, as long as they are also maintained in a tenancy by the entirety bank account.

Upon divorce, tenancy by the entirety automatically converts to tenants in common.

JOINT TENANCY   Joint tenancy is similar to tenants by the entirety but the co-owners are not married. Joint tenancy includes the common law right of survivorship, provided it is set out in the deed. Upon death of a joint tenant, title remains in the surviving joint tenant without further action. You can't leave joint tenancy property to someone else in your will.

There are some important differences. Joint tenants are not married so they are not treated as one legal entity. One owner may petition the court to divide the property or order its sale. A judgment creditor may also petition the court to divide the property and collect the judgment from one of the owner's shares.

JOINT OWNERSHIP AGREEMENTS   The law presumes equal ownership unless there is a written agreement specifying otherwise. All joint tenants and tenants in common, even if they are equal, should have a written joint ownership agreement. That agreement will define their interests in the property and the division of profits, tax benefits, expenses and responsibilities. It will establish the duration for the co-ownership. The agreement will also limit the right of one to sell or lease his share without the other's permission.

Consult with a real estate attorney for assistance. Joint ownership agreements are not expensive but can save substantial heartache later.

EQUITY SHARING & JOINT OWNERSHIP

Tenants – Would you like to own a home of your own? Are you tired of paying rent for someone else's mortgage? Don't have enough saved for a down payment? Having trouble qualifying for a new loan?

Investors – Worried tenants might abuse your property? Do maintenance, management and move - out headaches scare you? Are you reluctant to take on negative cash flows because rent will not cover the monthly cost of the mortgage?

Parents – Would you like to help the kids buy a house without committing to make a gift of the down payment?

Consider joint ownership. The occupant benefits by receiving part ownership of the property and all the tax advantages that go with it. The investor knows the occupant, as a part owner, will take care of the property and is unlikely to default. There is no negative cash flow on the investment. In most cases the purchase can qualify for favorable owner-occupied financing. Both the occupant and investor receive financial advantages over a traditional landlord tenant relationship.

THE HISTORY   Before 1981, tax laws considered property as a personal residence if any one of the owners lived in it. The non-resident could not treat his portion of the property as an investment and deduct costs such as depreciation, insurance or condominium fees. Only normal personal residence deductions such as interest and taxes were permitted. Depreciation was a major incentive to real estate investors as it allowed them to shelter other income from tax. It made no sense to participate in a joint ownership with a resident because the investor could not take depreciation. Simply put, the returns were much higher if you were a 100% investor owner.

Tax law changes in 1981 allowed a part - owner, investor, to take depreciation on property occupied by another part - owner. The new law required a written shared equity financing agreement often abbreviated to SEFA. Hence the name "Equity Sharing" evolved.

HOW EQUITY SHARING WORKED   Usually, the investor made the down payment for the purchase and the occupant paid the entire monthly mortgage payment. Since the occupant didn't own all the property, a portion of the occupant's monthly payment was rent for his use of the investor's portion of the property. The amount was determined by figuring the fair market rent for the home. If the occupant owned half of the home, then a portion of the mortgage payment equal to half of the fair market rent was rent. As rent it was not deductible to the occupant and considered income to the investor.

The occupant received a partial write-off of his share of the interest and taxes. The investor got the write-off for half the depreciation. Income from the rent was close to equal his obligation on the interest, taxes and condo fees so the investor usually had no income to tax. When the property sold, the parties would split the profit.

A fairly standard formula determined the division of ownership. A 20% down payment would entitle the investor to 50% ownership. The basis for this division was the observation that a 40% down payment would buy an investment property with no negative cash flow; the rent would equal the mortgage payment, taxes and insurance. If you have no negative, because the occupant is making all the payment, you should only own half the property for half the normally required down payment. (If 40% down equals 100% ownership, then 20% down equals 50% ownership)

Equity Sharing benefited the investor because there was no negative cash flow. The investment carried little risk because it had none of the headaches and uncertainties facing a landlord: maintenance, management and move-outs. Assuming modest appreciation rates of 5% per year, annual returns for the investor of 14% were common.

The occupant usually gained $200 to $300 per month over his position as a tenant. Even though the occupant's monthly payment was more than he would have paid in rent, his share of the appreciation in value more than paid that back.

TAX LAW CHANGES Changes to the tax laws beginning in 1986 severely limited the depreciation deduction by lengthening the useful life for residential property to over 30 years. In addition, there are limits on the use of passive losses to offset other income. Losses from activities such as real estate investment are passive losses. High income taxpayers may find themselves unable to deduct depreciation at all.

THE NEW EQUITY SHARING A new form of equity sharing has emerged looking more like a traditional partnership. It is a voluntary return to the pre-1981 tax treatment. The investor still makes the down payment and the occupant pays the mortgage and closing costs. However, the investor foregoes the depreciation deduction and allows the occupant to take the entire write-off for interest and taxes. None of the occupant's payment is rent. When the property sells, the investor is repaid and the profit is split.

This is not equity sharing in the traditional sense of the word. In fact, it may be dangerous from a tax standpoint to refer to the arrangement as equity sharing!

If the IRS treats the arrangement as equity sharing under the SEFA regulations, the occupant loses the full deduction for interest and taxes. The IRS will treat a part of the monthly payment as rent. The investor must then recognize the rental income. He paid none of the mortgage payment, so he would have no deduction for interest and real estate taxes to offset the income. The investor would owe tax with no cash in his pocket. Avoid use of the term "equity sharing." Call the agreement a "joint ownership agreement."

THE DIVISION OF OWNERSHIP   The new joint ownership brought about a new formula for division of ownership. The investor's 20% down payment is no longer equal to a 50% ownership interest. Now, the investor receives his 50% interest for only a 10% down payment. The occupant pays closing costs and all the monthly payment. The occupant now has a full write-off for the entire mortgage payment. Often the investor does not co-sign on the loan so his only risk is the down payment. This is a very attractive arrangement for the investor. Annual returns of 20% or more are possible.

THE OCCUPANT'S POSITION   Where does the occupant stand?   Under certain circumstances, the new equity sharing is not good for the occupant unless real estate appreciates at very high rates. Here's what to watch out for.
Look for property that is bargain priced. You are counting on future appreciation to repay the investor and realize a profit. Serious real estate investors will tell you, "You make money when you buy property, not when you sell it."

In all cases, the occupant will pay more on a monthly basis than the cost to rent the property. That is because the payment of principal, interest, taxes and insurance on a 90% loan will usually be more than rent. Income tax deductions for interest and real estate taxes will soften the blow. In addition to a higher mortgage payment, the occupant pays for most maintenance that normally is a landlord's responsibility. Repainting, landscaping, and appliance repairs are expensive but often ignored in projections. Many equity share agreements provide the investor will participate in major repairs.

The occupant hopes that his share of the appreciation will be enough to repay this deficiency together with his closing costs and the costs of sale. Obviously, the longer the agreement runs, the better the occupant's chances of making a profit.

The method of defining and dividing profit is even more important than the length of the agreement. The new joint ownership agreements fall into two broad groups dividing either the equity or the profit.

DIVIDING EQUITY   Some agreements divide the equity in the property. These do not repay the occupant his closing costs or the principal amortization. The investor receives a return of the down payment, then the loan is paid off, then the equity in the property is split.

Such agreements do not generally favor the occupant. The occupant will not receive enough to reimburse the original closing costs, rent deficiency and costs of sale unless, they run for longer than five years and real estate appreciates at high rates.

The property must appreciate by twice the amount of these costs because the occupant only gets half the appreciation. Otherwise, he would be better off renting. That would take sustained appreciation of 6% per year for a five year agreement. With a three year agreement, the required appreciation rate would be 10% per year. Real estate must appreciate at rates above this, year after year, without fail, for the occupant to be ahead of the tenant with a savings account.

DIVIDING PROFIT   Other joint ownership agreements reimburse the occupant for the mortgage amortization, then the investor for his down payment, then the occupant for the closing costs. The remaining profit is split. These agreements are much more favorable to the occupant without diminishing the investor's return to unacceptable levels.

OTHER JOINT OWNERSHIP AGREEMENTS   Joint ownership agreements are not limited to equity sharing type arrangements between an investor and an occupant. Any time two unmarried individuals acquire an interest in property they should have a written joint ownership agreement. The agreement should address the division of ownership, down payment and monthly payment. It will also define responsibility for repairs, how to treat improvements, default, and sale. The agreement will set out the terms of a future sale or lease of the property.

Not all agreements are alike. Consult with your attorney and tax advisor before entering into any joint ownership agreement.

A sample Joint Ownership Agreement can be found in Section Five

FINANCING

HOW TO ATTRACT BUYERS TO YOUR HOUSE - WHY LOWERING YOUR PRICE MAY BE A MISTAKE

OVERCOMING THE OBSTACLES   There are three major obstacles for all buyers. They are lack of a sufficient down payment, high monthly payments, and problems qualifying.

DOWN PAYMENT   Many agents and individuals overlook potential sources of down payment. It is possible to borrow against income tax refunds, IRA and retirement accounts, stocks or bonds. Anything that can be appraised is potential collateral for a loan. Coin and gun collections are examples.

If a loan is not practical, maybe you can sell an asset to a relative with the understanding you may buy it back later. That does not create a debt and does not appear as an obligation for other qualifying purposes. Neither does borrowing the cash value of a life insurance policy.

Co-ownership is another potential source of down payment. Joint ownership with family members is a viable solution. Parents provide the down payment and the children carry the mortgage. When the property sells, the family splits the profits. Parent/investors receive tax benefits offsetting other income. If they live out of town, trips back to see the children become business trips to inspect their investment and may be tax deductible also.

Some loans allow gift letters to provide closing costs and down payments. Be sure of your gift letters. Under many contracts, the buyer can be in default if the benefactor changes his mind and does not fund the gift.

MONTHLY PAYMENTS   The best way to lower monthly payments, attract and qualify buyers is interest rate buy downs rather than price reductions. Consider a $100,000, 80% loan at 7.5% interest. For every $1000 of price reduction the buyer saves $200 down and his loan is $800 less. That saves him $7.02 per month on his payment. A 3-2-1 interest rate buy down reduces the rate 3 points the first year, two the second and one the third. The same $1000 applied to a 3-2-1 interest rate buydown saves $154 per month in cash the first year, $105 the second and $54 the third.

These numbers become more significant when applied to higher loans. Assume the house is listed for $210,000 and the seller will accept $200,000. The $10,000 price reduction on a 90% loan at 7.5% translates to $1000 less down but only reduces the monthly payment $63 per month. The same $10,000 will more than fund a 3-2-1 buy down and reduce the payment $345 per month the first year. That is the equivalent of a $20,000 raise for qualifying purposes.

Also available is a 2-1 buy down. These cost approximately 2.6% of the loan amount. To save $200 per month on a $100,000 house would require a $25,000 price reduction. A 2-1 buy down with a 20% down payment saves the same amount for only $2400.

Alternatively, the $10,000 would fund a permanent 1% reduction in the interest rate. Savings to the buyer would be $134 per month or $48,240 over the thirty year loan life.

Low rates may be available on ARMs but they do not afford the certainty of a buy down. An ARM might increase six points over its life while a 3-2-1 buy down only goes up three points. Often, first year rates are lower with the buy down.

The entire amount of the buy-down can be tax deductible for the buyer in the year paid. This may generate a significant saving for the buyer. The fact the seller reimburses the buyer does not take away the deduction.

There are limits on buy down funds and the rules change often. Check with your lender before committing.

INCREASING THE BUYER'S QUALIFICATIONS Buy downs dramatically affect the buyer's qualifying. An income of $75,000 per year qualifies for a $193,000 conventional level payment loan. A 3-2-1 buydown increases buying power an additional $40,000 to a loan of $234,000. If the seller won't pay the buy down, it makes sense for the buyer to do so. Lender funded buy downs are also available.

Changing loan programs may also increase borrowing power. Forty percent of potential buyers are either veterans or married to one. Income of $45,000 allows a VA loan of $140,000 versus a conventional loan of only $115,000. The VA graduated payment program boosts borrowing power to $170,000.

Additional down payment is another way to increase the buyer's qualifying power. Lender's allow higher debt to income ratios with larger down payments. Between reducing the loan amount and increasing the ratio, an additional $5000 down can increase the loan qualification $25,000. Borrowing $5,000 from other sources such as cash value in a life insurance policy looks very smart.

Some loans allow higher debt ratios if the house is rated as energy efficient.

QUALIFYING THE BUYER Pre-qualify the buyer and obtain a credit report. Almost 20% of all credit reports contain erroneous and detrimental information. Getting the report early gives you time to correct the errors. In addition, the buyer may not have told you the truth about his financial picture. Having the report early avoids last minute surprises.

REHABILITATING CREDIT If you suspect an error on your credit report, you have important rights under the Fair Credit Reporting Act. Challenge the incorrect information. The reporting agency must notify the creditor of your inquiry. If the creditor does not respond within 30 days, the agency must remove the detrimental information. If the creditor insists the information is correct, you may place a 100 word explanation in your credit file. That explanation will accompany all future reports.

A bankruptcy does not necessarily bar future credit. FHA specifically provides a business related bankruptcy does not affect the application for credit. Other loans may be available on a case by case basis after 2 to 3 years if the bankrupt has cleaned up his credit and had no additional problems. Mitigating factors include bankruptcy caused by medical emergency, divorce or loss of job.

ASSUMPTION TRANSACTIONS Popular belief is that assumptions are all but dead. They are not. VA and FHA loans are assumable and even conventional loans can be taken over through use of an installment land contract. See the Article in this Section on How to Assume the Non-Assumable Loan.

If the seller can no longer make the payments, lenders would prefer an assumption to a foreclosure. You should ask.

ADVERTISE TERMS NOT PRICE REDUCTIONS Agents and sellers should learn from the car dealers. People don't buy cars or houses based on price. They want to know, "How much a month?" Recognizing this, consider buy downs and other means to lower the monthly payment and dramatically increase the buyer's borrowing power.

However, you should use general statements when advertising. Don't mention specific interest rates or payments and you'll avoid extensive truth in lending disclosures required by Regulation Z.

CONTRACTS FOR DEED - HOW TO ASSUME THE NON-ASSUMABLE LOAN

Subprime lending woes have led to a credit crunch that makes qualifying for new loans much more difficult. The good news is, "Buyers don't need a new loan!" Its time to dust off a trick from the past and learn how to move property using the existing loan. If you've shied away from Contracts for Deed in the past, read on. There are new and close-to-foolproof ways to avoid the Due on Sale Clause that protecs the Buyer and leaves nothing on the public record to indicate a transfer has taken place. Here's how the new Secured Contract for Deed answers today's problems for both buyers and sellers.

DISCLAIMER This article is written for general information only. It is based on English Common Law and the law of Virginia. Other states may have different rules. Be sure to check with a local real estate attorney for an interpretation of the law in your jurisdiction.

THE SELLER'S SQUEEZE When credit tightens and demand softens, Sellers are squeezed two ways.

1.   High inventory means Sellers must offer something to make their house stand out from the crowd.

2.   Lower prices mean homes might not appraise for enough to pay off the Seller's old 100% loan and costs of sale. Short sales are not always an option because of tax consequences or lack of "hardship."

THE BUYER'S SQUEEZE Tighter credit also squeezes Buyers.

1. Buyers may be capable of paying the loan but are never given a chance because they don't fit a lender's profile. One hard-to-finance group is the credit challenged including newly employed persons, immigrants, the self-employed and those with recent job changes. Another is the credit impaired such as those with bankruptcies, foreclosures, short-sales, divorces, high student loans, or alimony.

2. Investors and self-employeds are a big part of the market but investor and stated income loans are gone. Many well-qualified people cannot get a loan.

THE CONTRACT FOR DEED ANSWER The Contract for Deed is a method of private financing where the Buyer takes over the Seller's payments. The Seller retains title to the property until the Buyer has paid the purchase price in full. It is similar to buying on lay-away except the Buyer takes possession of the property and enjoys the benefits of ownership, including all income tax deductions for interest and property taxes.

CONTRACT FOR DEED ADVANTAGES

1. The low interest rate loan stays in place. No new qualifying, no increase in monthly payment.

2. Qualifying is as easy as the Seller wants it to be. Forget inaccurate and inconsistent credit scoring.

3. Closing costs are considerably less because there are no lender processing or mortgage recording fees. Junk fees have no place here!

4. Buyers are interested. No lender hassles. Quick settlement.

5. Flexible financing. Terms, payment and rates are negotiable.

HOW DOES IT WORK? At settlement, the Seller executes a Deed to the Buyer. The Buyer pays the balance of the down payment and closing costs and executes a Note payable to the Seller. The buyer takes possession of the property. Both parties sign the Contract for Deed and related escrow agreements.

So far, the transaction looks like a regular settlement. The difference is: instead of a new loan, we record a Security Deed of Trust (or mortgage) against the property. Va Code Section 55-58.1. This Deed of Trust secures the Buyer preventing the Seller's creditors from asserting an interest ahead of the Buyer. It also secures the Seller against the Buyer's default and assures the Buyer an income tax deduction for the mortgage interest.

The settlement agent holds the Deed and Note in escrow until the Buyer pays off the loan through a sale or refinancing. Then, the Deed is recorded vesting full title in the Buyer. The Seller signed all necessary documents at the first closing. It does not matter if he later moves from the area, dies or is otherwise unavailable.

The Buyer makes monthly payments which are used to pay the existing loan with any left-over going to the Seller. This is sometimes called a wrap-around contract because the second loan "wraps around" or includes the first. On-line banking makes it easy for the Buyer to send the payment directly (and anonymously) to the lender. Both parties can check on-line to be sure the payments are made on time.

WRAP AROUND LOANS   Wrap around loans are very flexible. The parties can agree on a loan term different from the existing loan. For example, the wrap around could be written as due in 5 years even though the underlying loan has 25 years left to go.

If the Buyer does not have enough down payment to pay the Sellers their equity, the Seller could accept a smaller down payment and defer receiving the rest of the money until the loan is paid off. The wrap around is written for more than the existing loan.

In addition, the Seller can realize a profit on the financing by charging the Buyer a higher interest rate than he pays on the existing financing. For example, if the existing loan is $300,000 at 6%, the Seller pays $18,000 per year in interest. If he charges the Buyer 7%, he receives $21,000 for a $3,000 profit each year. Over 5 years the profit is $15,000. This is an incentive for the Seller to accept a lower selling price. A lower sale price makes the Buyer happy and reduces the cash down payment.

Alternatively, the Seller might offer the incentive of a lower payment than the existing loan. The Contract could be written with interest-only or graduated payments. The Seller would make up the difference – similar to renting with a negative but without the ownership responsibilities.

The combination of low down payment and flexible financing without formal application makes the Contract for Deed very attractive to both buyers and sellers.

INSURANCE   The Seller adds the Buyer to the Seller's homeowner's insurance policy as an "additional insured" to protect the Buyer's interest. The Seller will need to convert the policy to a non-owner occupied policy like a landlord's. They Buyer would need a policy to cover his personal belongings and liability.

CONTRACT FOR DEED PRECAUTIONS   Most loans (all, except VA loans) contain what is known as a Due on Sale Clause giving the lender an option to call the loan due if any interest in the property is transferred.   This is also referred to as "accelerating" the loan. Contracts for Deed, Lease Options and Land Trusts all trigger the due-on-sale clause. There is no magic bullet to avoid the Due on Sale Clause. This means there is a possibility the lender may discover the transaction and call the loan due. If this happens, the Buyer must refinance at current interest rates and terms. If the Buyer can not qualify for a new loan, foreclosure may result.   However, the risk of discovery is very low with a Secured Contract for Deed because the Contract is not recorded and there is nothing on the public record to evidence a transfer.

While we cannot guarantee the lender will not call the loan, our experience is that lender's do not seem to notice or care -- so long as the Buyer keeps the payments current. There is little financial incentive for the lender to call the loan because interest rates have remained relatively low and lenders already have their hands full with foreclosures. A servicing lender has no incentive to call the loan and risk losing the servicing income.

Are these arrangements illegal? No. Violating the due-on-sale clause is not against the law. It gives the lender the option to call the loan.

ADVANTAGES FOR THE SELLER

1.   No appraisal

2.   No financing contingency to worry about

3.   Wider range of potential buyers

4.   Possible profit on financing – make up for a lower price by charging a higher interest rate than the existing loan with "wrap around" financing

5.   Quicker settlement (no waiting for lender approval).

RISK TO THE SELLER

1.   The Seller remains liable on the loan until it is paid either through a refinance or sale of the property.   If the loan is called it will reflect on the Seller. To protect the Seller, many Contracts for Deed provide that upon default, the Buyer's interest terminates and all sums previously paid are rent. The Seller can evict the Buyer and take the property back.

2.   The loan continues on the Seller's credit report. This could present issues for the Seller to qualify on a new home. Most lenders will count at least 75% of the Buyer's payment as income to the Seller for qualifying purposes.   Of course, if the Seller uses a Contract for Deed to buy his next house, this is not an issue.

3.   This risk of non-payment is similar to the risk assumed by any landlord. The contract for deed has an advantage over a lease because the Buyer is paying the full cost of the mortgage, homeowner fees and maintenance. In addition, the Buyer has paid closing costs and has an ownership interest. Unlike a lease, there should be no maintenance, management and move-out hassles.

4.   The Buyer never goes through a formal application process. Sellers should insist on accurate and complete credit information. Ask to see a copy of

the credit report and tax returns. Pay a friendly mortgage lender to evaluate the application. Insist on a reasonable down payment under the circumstances.

ADVANTAGES FOR THE BUYER

1.   No loan qualifying

2.   Low or flexible down payment

3.   Favorable interest rates and flexible terms

4.   Lower closing costs

5.   Quicker settlement (no waiting for lender approval).

RISK TO THE BUYER

1.   Three to five years is a minimum recommended time for a refinance. That gives time for the property to appreciate and the buyer to earn more money or resolve credit issues to qualify for a refinance

2.   If the Buyer defaults, the Contract for Deed terminates the buyer's interest upon default, and treats all payments as rent and the Buyer could stand to lose his investment.

3.   A lender who discovers the transaction may call the loan immediately due and payable. If the Buyer can't qualify for financing, foreclosure may result and the Buyer could lose the benefit of his investment.

COSTS TO CLOSE   Even with the additional attorney fees to prepare the Contract for Deed documents, the total closing costs are less than a new loan because there are no lender fees, no duplicate recording fees for a Deed and Deed of Trust and a survey is not required. The parties usually choose to split the attorney fees. Other closing costs including settlement and recording fees remain the same as a regular closing. Settlement can be quick because there is no loan application to process. It usually takes only a week for a title search and to obtain loan and escrow balance information.

LIKELY BUYER PROSPECTS

Those with less than stellar credit (but explainable – divorce, job loss, etc.)

Foreclosure or short sale victims (strongARMed out of their last house)

Those with low down payments (Don't have 20% but want to avoid PMI)

Investors

LIKELY SELLER PROSPECTS

Expired listings ("I know something your last agent didn't tell you about.")

Want to sell but don't need to buy (Investors, transfers, divorce, burnouts)

Don't qualify for a short sale (can't prove hardship)

Bad tax consequences (don't qualify for exclusion of forgiven debt)

HOW DO YOU DO IT? Prepare a Sales Contract using a Seller Financing Addendum to set out the terms. Specify a "Wrap Around Contract for Deed."

Then, fill in the payment terms required by the balance of the paragraph. If the loan is adjustable, be sure to spell out the terms.

If you want to utilize Contract for Deed financing, get qualified professionals to advise and protect you.

If needed, add a contingency "This Contract is contingent upon the parties receiving an explanation of Contract for Deed financing from an attorney of their choice. This contract shall be null and void if this contingency is not removed by 6 PM on (date)." Allow five days to be safe.

HOW TO PAYOFF FHA LOANS

Most borrowers believe there is no prepayment penalty on an FHA loan. In fact, there can be a substantial penalty. You can avoid most of this penalty.

The lender may require that payoff of an FHA loan be on a "due date." Due dates are on the first of the month. Suppose a payoff was on the 10th. The lender could collect interest all the way through to the next due date, the first of the following month.

In addition, the FHA lender may also require notice of the prepayment at least 30 days before the due date. Suppose the lender received a payoff during May. The lender received no other notice the loan would pay off early. The lender could collect interest for the entire month of May and June. The lender did not receive notice of payment more than 30 days before the next due date of June 1. Two months of additional interest is roughly a 1.6% prepayment penalty.

When listing a house for sale, you should notify the lender of the potential for a prepayment. Send another letter to the lender (certified mail, return receipt requested) to arrive during the month before settlement. Some lenders want the borrower to sign the notice. Be careful - some lenders specify an address for correspondence which is different from the address used for payments. Check the payment book or coupons carefully.

Notify the settlement agent that the Seller has an FHA loan to payoff. Check to verify they can process all papers for the payoff to arrive before the end of the month of settlement. If necessary, move the settlement earlier in the month to allow sufficient time. Usually this means you should schedule settlement no later than the 25th of the month.

HOW TO AVOID THE PROBLEM SETTLEMENT

This article was written for real estate agents. The advice applies to buyers and sellers as well.

It's bound to happen, sooner or later. You find yourself with a settlement that is not going to be easy. You wonder if the case will settle at all. You can avoid most of these situations. Avoiding surprises is the key ingredient to smooth and successful settlements. Surprises usually result from lack of preparation.

At each stage of the contract and settlement process you can remain in control by preparing the parties. How you handle these stages will determine how settlement will proceed.

THE LISTING You can avoid many problems at the listing stage. First, the seller should clearly understand the marketing plan and listing agreement. Explain what they should expect of you and what you expect of the seller.

You should carefully check the chattels included in the listing. If the seller plans on moving or replacing certain items, remove them from the house or clearly mark them. Describe the appliances accurately. Is it a heat pump or a regular air conditioner with an electric furnace? Is the oven self cleaning or continuous cleaning? Identify and mark any items that are to convey "as is."

Check the property for potential surprises. Is it really wall to wall carpet or is it an area rug the seller is taking with him? Be careful of the statement "hardwood floors" if not all areas have them. Does the central air conditioning service the whole house? Most states obligate you to disclose promptly any material information that is reasonably available to you. Avoid surprises. Ask questions.

Ask the seller to check and sign the property data sheet you use to collect information for the listing. That way the seller is certifying the information, not you. Don't rely on the county records to determine if a property is on public water and sewer. Those records are not always accurate.

Ask the seller for a copy of their deed and survey. Use them to check the proper legal description and verify who is on the title. Ask if there have been any deaths, divorces or remarriages.

The seller should be ready to deliver the home in broom clean condition. Check the warranty provisions of your contract. Most require the appliances, heating, air conditioning, plumbing etc. be in working order at the time of settlement. Encourage the seller to repair any questionable items when you take the listing. That will avoid escrows later.

Advise ordering termite, radon, home, well and septic inspections at the time of listing. This lets you and the seller know where the problems are and avoids last minute surprises. A satisfactory report may convince the buyer he does not need to make his contract contingent on another inspection. If you do order early remember that some inspections expire and will need to be updated before settlement.

Most wells fail the first inspection and many public health agencies require septic fields be in active use for thirty days before an inspection. If the house is vacant, the seller must escrow money until the buyer has lived there for thirty days pending a satisfactory inspection.

VA, FHA, and ARM loans may all be assumable but the conditions vary widely. Do not rely on your memory or the seller's. Check with the lender for all requirements and fees. If the Veteran seller expects a release of liability or reinstatement, be sure that is in the listing agreement and the contract.

THE BUYER Avoid dual agency. Be sure the buyer understands your agency disclosure form. Get it signed and in your file. Pre-qualify buyers for their loans. Get a lender's preliminary opinion letter but don't let the parties mistake it for a loan commitment.

Buyers should understand, in most states, there is no cooling off period in most states after signing a contract. The deposit is not the sole limit of their liability if they default.

Review the list of chattels carefully. If the item is on the listing, it is offered for sale. If it is not in the contract, it is not sold.

Explain that a home conveys in "as is" not new condition. Broken windows, door locks, carpet stains and leaky basements may not be fixed unless the seller agrees in the contract. If the buyer expresses concern about the property condition, you may suggest an inspection without violating your duty to the seller. That information will help sell the house. Do not try to talk a buyer out of an inspection. If a problem arises later, you will be blamed.

THE CONTRACT The contract should be legible, the math checked, and all of the information correct and accurate. Use plain English and avoid the use of ambiguous terms such as "satisfactory." If you must use a contingency be sure to state it in clear terms. Spell out IF something happens, BY a certain time, THEN what.

Get the contract and all addendums to the settling attorney and lender as soon as possible.

Be sure the seller knows he must be out of the house on the day of settlement. Even better, the seller should be completely out in time for the walk-through inspection. Coordinate the transfer of utilities so that they will be turned on for the walk-through.

THE SETTLEMENT Let the settlement attorney know if any of the parties will not be at settlement. Watch out for Powers of Attorney. They are complex legal documents and most forms prepared outside you state may not be acceptable. The seller can use a power of attorney to sign most settlement documents but usually not the deed. Title insurance companies impose his requirement to protect against fraud and forgery.

If the purchaser plans to use a power of attorney the lender will need to review and approve it.

Use a professional settlement attorney. Recommend someone who is not afraid to take a position and resolve disputes. A firm hand will dispose of most problems.

Avoid settling on the 15th or 30th of the month. They are the busiest days and the slightest problem may delay the case. If you know you've got a problem discuss it with the attorney ahead of time. They don't like surprises either!

DISBURSEMENT Be sure the seller understands your local practice. In many states the Seller's proceeds are not disbursed at the table. This allows for clearance of the purchaser's funds and loan proceeds as well as recordation of documents. Keep this in mind when planning coinciding settlements as many title companies will not accept an assignment of funds.

HOW TO SPOT AND AVOID RESPA VIOLATIONS

The Real Estate Settlement Procedures Act (RESPA) became law in 1974. Section 2 (a) tells why: "The Congress finds that significant reforms in the real estate settlement process are needed to insure that consumers throughout the Nation are provided with greater and more timely information on the nature and costs of the settlement process and are protected from unnecessarily high settlement charges caused by certain abusive practices that have developed in some areas of the country."

Section 8 of RESPA prohibits the payment of kickbacks and unearned fees for business referrals. Section 8 also regulates abuses associated with controlled business arrangements.

RESPA languished for many years with little enforcement effort but that changed as complaints of RESPA violations mounted. HUD has formed a RESPA enforcement unit which is investigating and prosecuting abuses. Many agents and brokers are violating RESPA without realizing the dire consequences.

ANTI-KICKBACK PROVISIONS The Act provides that "No person shall give and no person shall accept any fee, kickback, or thing of value pursuant to any agreement or understanding, oral or otherwise, that business incident to or a part of a real estate settlement service... shall be referred to any person." The law defines a "thing of value" broadly. It can include any payment, advance, fund, loan, service or other consideration. Ordinary and customary business courtesies, lunches and promotions are probably insignificant and are unlikely to result in prosecution. Other violations may be less obvious but illegal. Where will HUD draw the line?

According to written opinion letters from HUD, providing or accepting sports tickets, vacation trips, use of a beach condo, fax machines, computers, mailing services or contributions to the company's advertising fund are all violations. So are excessive business gifts or gifts tied to the number of settlements or loans sent to a particular firm. Offering or accepting prizes to the broker or agent who refers the most business violates Section 8. A raffle in which the agent receives one chance for each referral is illegal. Agents receiving free legal services or settlements are violating the law.

If the agent or company is paid the commission at settlement, provided they use a particular settlement service, that is a violation if such payment not normal in the area,. According to HUD, the fact they were paid early is a thing of value, given to induce them to refer business.

An indirect payment is also illegal. Suppose a title company contributes to a company's advertising fund for each settlement referred. That indirectly benefits the agent and company. The agent, the company and the title company are all violating RESPA. Both the giver and the receiver are equally guilty and HUD prosecutes both. In one case, HUD also invited the IRS to participate. Because the agent who received the "thing of value" did not include it in income for the year, criminal tax fraud prosecution resulted.

Real estate agents or their companies can legitimately expect to receive good service for their clients and customers. Anything an agent or broker receives as an inducement to refer business potentially violates RESPA.

PAYMENT FOR SERVICES PERFORMED   RESPA does not prohibit all payments but does contain a narrow exception for services actually performed. The fees cannot be excessive and cannot be for work the person would frequently or normally do as part of their job. For example, a settlement agent could not pay the agent for ordering a termite inspection if the agent does that anyway.

One of the examples in the RESPA regulations mentions a lender paying the agent a fee for arranging for the appraiser to visit the property. The fee is for services that a real estate agent frequently performs without additional charge. The fee is really to compensate the agent for referring business. It is illegal. The agent is also guilty. To be legal, the services must be substantial and justify the size of the fee.

If a settlement agent does nothing more than refer business to another company that does all the work and shares fees, it violates RESPA. The fees paid must bear a reasonable relationship to the value of the services.

Another example from the regulations:

"Facts: A, a real estate broker, obtains all necessary licenses under state law to act as a title insurance agent. A refers individuals who are purchasing homes in transactions in which A participates as a broker to B, a title company, for the purchase of title insurance services. A fills out a simple form but performs no other services in connection with the issuance of the title insurance policy. B pays A a commission for the transaction.

Comments: The payment of a commission by B to A under circumstances where no substantial services are being provided by A to B is a violation of Section 8 of RESPA."

Many of the sub-agency relationships set up between brokers and title companies violate RESPA. If the real estate company has a settlement service, that exists in name only, you should question the relationship. Ask how much the company's settlement service firm receives and what work it actually does to receive the payment. HUD will be asking those very questions. If the payment seems excessive in relation to the work or if it is for work that would normally be done anyway, without extra payment, the real estate company, the settlement company and the title company are guilty of criminal RESPA violations.

CONTROLLED BUSINESS Another abusive practice RESPA attacks is controlled business. A controlled business arrangement is a system in which a person refers or affirmatively influences referrals to a provider in which he has an interest. A provider could be a settlement agent, lender, termite company, or insurance agent. Direct or indirect ownership or influence are all covered. Ownership of only 1% of a company is enough of an interest. If your company has its own settlement service or mortgage company, it is a controlled business arrangement.

REPSA regulates but does not prohibit controlled business completely. If you are in a controlled business arrangement, you must do three things. First, when you refer someone to a related company, disclose your relationship and provide a written estimate of the expected charges. Second, you cannot require or coerce the buyer to heed your recommendation. You must inform the buyer of his right to select others. Don't pressure the buyer so he feels required to use your provider. Third, you can not receive any direct or indirect "thing of value" from the provider for the referral. That would violate the anti-kickback provisions. Dividends as a return on your ownership interest in the provider are permissible. Dividends based on how much business you refer are not.

Be sure you follow the three requirements outlined above. Because of the great potential for abuse, HUD will scrutinize controlled business arrangements carefully. Be certain that any payment from one company to the other does not violate anti-kickback rules.

PENALTIES RESPA violations are criminal acts carrying a fine of not more than $10,000 or imprisonment for not more than one year. In addition, RESPA charges violators of the controlled business regulations three times the amount paid. Violate the anti-kickback rules, and you are liable for three times the amount you collected. In all cases, the Court can assess court costs and attorney fees against you.

HUD also has an impressive arsenal of administrative remedies. If the transaction involves a conventional loan, HUD may bring an action to stop the activity and require the company to return all profits.

If the transaction involves an FHA loan, HUD may also bar the guilty party from further participation in FHA loan programs and impose additional civil penalties of double damages and a $5,000 fine. A HUD investigation may open the offending firm and individuals to civil class action suits from aggrieved consumers. The costs of defending these actions are enormous. An agent's malpractice policy won't cover violation of a criminal law. The state regulatory commission may add its own disciplinary sanctions to the agent's troubles.

In addition to RESPA, an agent who steers a buyer to a company owned settlement service is asking for dual agency claims and ethical complaints. Advising the buyer on where to go for settlement is as dangerous as telling him he doesn't need a home inspection.

WHAT SHOULD AN AGENT DO?   RESPA violations are crimes. Don't take chances. If your company won't change, change companies. Don't steer or refer business unless you are sure you can justify the entire arrangement. Avoid even the appearance of impropriety. Receiving something of value is as bad as giving it and subjects you to the same fines and penalties. Don't accept referral fees, advertising donations, gifts, early disbursements or free services or machines. Don't participate in contests or raffles that promise you or your company returns for business referrals.

If you are in a controlled business arrangement, be sure to use the appropriate disclosures. Be ready to prove that you did. Have the buyer sign the written disclosure that RESPA requires. Recommend three choices other than the one related to you or your company. Don't pressure and don't succumb to pressure to refer business to a related company.

HUD SLAMS SHAMS

As a Broker, you're presented with a business opportunity. A title company or lender offers you a joint venture. They'll supply the expertise, you supply the customers. All you need do is refer buyers and you'll receive a part of the profits. Sound too good to be true?

Consider the following joint venture between a broker and title company: An existing real estate broker and an existing title insurance company form a joint venture. Each participant in the joint venture contributes $1000 towards the creation of the joint title agency. The title insurance company provides title searches and commitments at below cost. It also manages the joint venture that is located in the title company's offices. One employee of the title company is "leased" to the joint venture and continues to do the same work she did for the title insurance company. The real estate broker is the joint venture's sole source of business.

Regulations from HUD (effective June 7, 1996) conclude this is an example of an entity that is not a bona fide provider of settlement services. Profits distributed to the broker will be illegal kickbacks.

Background In 1974, Congress, enacted the Real Estate Settlement Procedures Act (RESPA), prohibiting kickbacks, referral fees or granting favors to obtain a referral for a real estate settlement service. Congress recognized that payment of referral fees, favors and kickbacks unnecessarily increased costs to consumers. The value of the favor influenced the referral more than the combination of quality and price. The additional cost of the referral arrangement added only expense, not service.

A "thing of value means any payment, advance, funds, loan, service or other consideration." Included in prohibited "things of value" would be a settlement service provider such as a title company paying commissions before recording documents. It would also include an understanding to steer business in return for a title company or lender paying for advertising or open-house lunches, and a broker favoring an agent with relocation referrals or a better office space. Knowing and willful violation of the Virginia law subjects both the provider, and the receiver, to criminal penalties of up to $1,000 for each violation.

The Joint Venture Exception There is a difference between a kickback and a legitimate joint marketing venture. A real estate broker and a title company or lender can enter into an agreement to jointly market loans or settlement services. They can share profits from the joint venture. The real estate broker refers buyers to the joint venture and receives a return for his investment in the business. These are controlled business arrangements.

HUD recognizes there can be legitimate controlled business arrangements. To quote from the regulations, "RESPA's anti-kickback provisions were not intended to prohibit the payments for goods furnished or services actually rendered, so long as the payment bears a reasonable relationship to the value of the goods or services received by the person or company making the payment. To the extent the payment is in excess of the reasonable value of the goods provided or services performed, the excess may be considered a kickback..."

Joint Venture Abuses   Controlled business can lead to two kinds of abuses. The most obvious is steering a consumer to the "company store" without regard for the best price or services. A joint venture controlled business presents a second regulatory challenge. The joint venture may be nothing more than an empty shell—sharing a fee, but adding no value to the transaction. Profit distributions from an empty shall are a disguised kickback to the joint owner who made the referral.

Sham Entities   HUD recognizes the joint venture can be a subterfuge, designed to look like a legitimate business. The sham joint venture does not operate a legitimate stand-alone business or supply any services other than to provide a conduit for payment to the referring broker. The joint venture receives a fee without performing substantial work and the broker receives a return on investment that is really a kickback for making a referral.
HUD has established a series of questions to distinguish a bona fide settlement service provider from a conduit for passing kickbacks to the referring party. A bona fide venture will show evidence of proper capitalization, independent management and the ability to operate a stand-alone business, independent of referrals from one of the owners.

Factors to Consider   Here are the questions that determine if HUD will consider the joint venture a "bona fide settlement service provider" and therefore eligible to charge fees and pay a return to its owners:
1. Does the new entity have sufficient initial capital and net worth, typical in the industry, to conduct the settlement service business for which it was created? Typical start-up costs for a legitimate title and escrow company might run between twenty-five and fifty thousand dollars. Did the broker contribute his fair share for his percentage of ownership? If not, he has received an ownership interest for his ability to refer business. If the broker received a loan while the other party provided cash, the broker received favorable treatment. Both are a prohibited thing of value paid the broker for the referral of business.

2. Is the new entity staffed with its own (rather than loaned or shared) employees to perform the services it provides? Shared employees are evidence the joint venture has no substance. The venture cannot stand and operate alone and is, therefore, a sham.

3. Does the new entity manage its business affairs or is it managed by the parent provider of the services? Management is an important indicator of responsibility and liability for a company's performance. If the joint venture has no management or is managed by a parent company, it is an empty shell.

4. Does the new entity have an office separate from the parent or pay fair market rent to the parent? Shared office space is evidence the entity has no substance or separate identity. Payment of above or below-market rent to a parent company is further evidence of a kickback.

5. Is the new entity providing substantial services in return for the fee charged and does it incur risks and receive rewards of comparable enterprises operating in the market? Charging a fee without providing a commensurate service over-charges the consumer and provides unearned profits for the joint venture. All business has risks and when one of the parent companies bears all the risk, the venture is a sham.

6. Does the new entity perform all the substantial services itself or does it contract out a substantial portion of the work? Contracting out a substantial portion of the necessary work would be further evidence the joint venture does no real business of its own. Its main purpose is to collect a fee for a referral.

7. If the joint venture does contract out work, does it do so from an independent third party or from the parent? If the parent company actually does the work, how can the joint venture claim to be providing a valuable service for its fee?

8. If work is contracted out, is it at a fair rate or is the entity paying less than fair rate? Contracting the work out to the parent at less than fair rates inflates the return to the joint venture owners and is evidence of a kickback.

9. Is the entity competing in the market place for other business or does it rely solely on referred business? A legitimate business would be expected to solicit and obtain other independent work. Relying solely on referrals from a related company shows the venture is not competitive. It does not provide a service commensurate with its fees.

10. Is the new entity sending business exclusively to one of the settlement service providers that created it? A captive market is not a free market and affords a substantial opportunity to over-charge the consumer. Exclusive dealing is strong evidence the venture has no legitimate stand-alone business purpose.

Applying the Test: HUD will look at the entire set of circumstances surrounding the joint venture. No one question disposes of the issue. Consider the example at the beginning of this article—the venture is undercapitalized, the title company provides management and office space, the sole employee is leased, all business comes from the broker, and the title company supplies most services not the venture. After examining a similar example in the new regulations, HUD concluded the venture was not a bona fide settlement service provider and any payments by the joint venture to the broker would be an illegal kickback.

More Requirements: HUD cautions, that even if the entity passes the sham rest, it still must meet other conditions to be a legal controlled business. There must be a written disclosure of the controlled business arrangement including an estimate of charges and an admonition that the services may be available cheaper elsewhere. The referring party may not require use of a particular provider of settlement services. Owners may only receive payments based on their percentage of ownership, not the number of referrals.

Criminal Penalties   RESPA violations carry severe civil and criminal penalties including treble damages, fines and jail terms. Enforcement can come from HUD, state or private action. Enforcement actions usually start as a result of rivals turning in their competition.

TITLE INSURANCE

Title insurance protects the ownership interest in property against liens, encumbrances, or claims effecting title. The insurance indemnifies against loss or damage as a result of a claim. It can also protect against a subsequent buyer's refusal to settle because of some matter which has not yet resulted in a claim. Lender's always want title insurance to cover their interest but coverage for the owner is optional.

THE LAND RECORDS Most states do not certify ownership by issuing a certificate like a car title. The tax records tell who the county believes owns a piece of property, but they are not guaranteed to be accurate or complete. For example, tax records do not show liens, easements or restrictions. Most states provide a uniform system of recording and indexing documents. The Clerk of the Court will record any notarized document that meets the requirements for margins and type size. The state and county give no opinion about the validity of the document or its legal meaning. They do not certify that signatures are genuine or that the party signing had legal capacity or authority.

The Clerk's office indexes the records on the basis of the grantor (seller) and grantee (buyer) names. The indexes refer to the deed book and page number where a particular document is recorded. The title examiner's job is to find and review all documents which are in the chain of title.

To search a title, start with the person you believe is the present owner. Then search in the index back to the time he acquired the property. You will find references to documents where he may have conveyed an interest in the property or placed a lien on it. Judgments, wills and financing statements have their own indexes. You must search these as well. Be careful to note any entries with similar names or possible misspellings as they may be your party. Then, read each document to see if and how it applies to the property in question. You must check each buyer and seller in the chain of title. Title in Virginia goes all the way back to the King of England, but as a practical matter, title examiners only search for sixty years.

A typical title examination may require review of dozens or even hundreds of documents. If one of the sellers is named John Smith, there could be thousands of references to that name. Possible variations, such as Jon or Smythe magnify the assignment considerably.

TYPES OF DEFECTS There are two types of title defects. Those that are a matter of public record, and those that are not. Defects of record are those that are apparent on the face of the document itself. Examples would be an expired notary commission or a mistake in the legal description of the property. Other examples include missed second trusts, liens or taxes owed to more than one jurisdiction such as a County and Town. A defective notary clause is easy to overlook as is a mistake in one of the calls in a metes and bounds legal description. Sometimes a condominium parking space conveys separately from the unit itself. The unit's legal description can be a full page long and the examiner may pass over the parking space designation.

Title examiners should find recorded defects because they are obvious from a review of the county land records. Human error, distractions, or lack of attention to detail might cause the examiner to miss a particular document reference. In the course of examining hundreds of documents, these errors are bound to occur.

The examiner might also misinterpret the meaning or effect of a document and conclude that it does not apply to the property. An easement put on a farm may be hard to locate when the property is subdivided into lots. Some of the older utility easements do not have detailed plats describing where they are to go. These are referred to as "wild easements."

Judgments can be especially tricky. Judgments get indexed by name and are a lien against all property in the county owned by that person. If the name is sufficiently similar to put one on notice of the judgment, it is a lien. The examiner might check John Smith and forget to look for Jon Smythe, Smyth, Smithe, etc.

The examiner might make a mistake in a conclusion of law. Suppose a husband and wife own property. In Virginia, a judgment filed against the husband normally would not affect the property because it is jointly owned as tenants by the entirety. But, suppose the wife dies and the husband later remarries. The judgment is now a lien even if he has conveyed it to himself and his new wife as tenants by the entirety. Another example: A husband and wife own property as tenants by the entirety. They convey it to a third party using two separate deeds, one for each of them. Does the property convey? No, tenants by the entirety must convey their interests together in the same document.

Title, in Virginia, derives from the King of England. As a practical matter, title examiners only search for sixty years. Other states differ, but what if the defect is old? Adverse possession does not always cure your title if the rightful owner is incompetent, absent, or incarcerated. If the rightful owner is the state, you can't get adverse possession at all.

What if the same property is carried under two different legal descriptions and with two different names? Consider this bizarre but true tale from our files. The names are changed for this telling.

In 1909, Mary Jones, of Baltimore, acquired a lot in Northern Virginia through her father's will. In 1929, she married and wrote to the Clerk of the County Court asking to have the name changed to her married name. The county added her married name to the tax records but didn't delete her maiden name. As a result, there were two tax bills, in two different names, with two slightly different descriptions each year for the same piece of property. Mary paid the bills, she received, but the other bills, sent to an old address, were neither received nor paid for 33 years.

In 1962 the county sold the land at a tax sale. Mary never visited the property but continued to pay her tax bills until she died in 1974. In 1975, her son decided to go look at Mary's property in Virginia. To his surprise, there was a house on the once- vacant lot. A 46 year old clerical error now threatened that homeowner. The County eventually admitted its mistake and offered to pay Mary's estate the value of the property. The innocent homeowner did not fare so well. He did not have title insurance and had to pay his own attorney fees of several thousand dollars to defend his home.

Tax records contain many errors. Consider the owner who was surprised there were delinquent taxes against her condominium unit. When she bought the property 6 years before, she had declined owner's title insurance as too expensive. She saved $75 but paid out $1200 in taxes with penalties and interest. The builder and settlement company she bought from were no longer in business. No one from the county could explain why she was not notified earlier.

DEFECTS THAT ARE NOT OF RECORD   No title examiner can discover an unrecorded defect. They are not evident on the face of the documents nor can they be found. These are more dangerous because they are impossible to discover when doing a title search. Non-record defects leave an uninsured homeowner with no recourse except against his seller.

These defects may be the result of innocent mistakes. The most common innocent defect is an improperly indexed document. If the document is not in the grantor/grantee index, you don't know to look for it in the deed books. Misspelled or similar names add to the confusion. The index may also refer you to an incorrect deed book and page number.

Other common defects are not so innocent. They include fraud, forgery, missing heirs, legal incompetence of a seller and undisclosed parties. These are also the most damaging because they usually have the potential to cause a complete forfeiture of title.

Here are some specific examples:

Forged deeds, mortgages, and certificates of satisfaction. A forged certificate of satisfaction would show that a loan was paid off when in fact it was not.

False impersonation of the true owner or spouse.

Instruments executed under fabricated, expired or revoked powers of attorney.

Deeds valid on their face but delivered after the death of the grantor or without consent. Deeds by persons who are minors, or of unsound mind, or executed under duress.

Defective acknowledgments taken by an unauthorized notary public or one whose commission has expired.

Deeds by persons described as single but who are, in fact, married.

Deeds from a bigamous couple - the second marriage is void.

Undisclosed divorce converting the property to tenants in common where it is subject to the claims of creditors.

Undisclosed heirs, and missing wills including wills discovered after probate of the first will.

Misinterpretation of wills, deeds, or trusts, that result in litigation later.

Unpaid estate and gift taxes.

Deeds to or from a corporation that has had its charter revoked.

Corporate acts that have not been properly authorized.

Recorded easements where the pipe or wires do not follow the designated route.

Failure to include all necessary parties or lack of proper jurisdiction over parties in any past litigation pertaining to the title.

Deeds from nonexistent entities or involving fictitious parties to conceal illegal activities.

Federal condemnation or seizure of the property.

Conveyances that are void, as a matter of public policy, such as to settle a gambling debt or payment to commit a crime.

THREE HORROR STORIES Here are three rather unusual, but true, tales from our files.

Case #1 - Brown sold a piece of property to Jones and took back a note that had no payments for three years. He then sold that note to an investor who never bothered to notify Jones. The investor never recorded any notice of the assignment in the land records. When Jones sold the property, Brown acted like he still held the note. Since he couldn't produce the actual note, he signed a lost note affidavit at closing stating that he was the holder of the note and that it had been lost. Brown took the payoff money and left town.

One year later, when the note came due, the investor surfaced and demanded payment. Since Brown and Jones were both long gone, the investor instituted foreclosure proceedings against the property. The title insurance company paid off the note for the new owner.

Case #2 - Smith was a foreign service officer who could be out of the country for several months at a time. When he bought his house, he put down $150,000 but declined to take owner's title insurance because the lender already had insurance. He paid over $500,000 for the property but wanted to save money.

On one trip back, he was astounded to see his home listed in a foreclosure ad. He had made all of his payments and the lender listed in the ad was not someone he recognized. The sale was in two days. Smith hired an attorney to file an injunction and stop the foreclosure.

Further investigation revealed the foreclosure to be a complete fraud. The deed of trust referenced in the advertisement did not exist and the lender's phone was an answering machine. These were con artists preying on vacant property by advertising it for sale. The scheduled auction was attended by 25 bidders, each with a $10,000 deposit check. The "lender," who by now realized the scam had been discovered, never showed up. If the sale had proceeded, the "lender" and the deposit would have left town never to be heard from again.

This case illustrates that even if your title is good, you can still be involved in claims. It cost Smith $2,500 in attorney fees to find out he and the potential bidders were the victims of a hoax. Since he had no title insurance, the loss was his.

Case #3 - A builder bought land from a developer subject to approval of a preliminary site plan by the county. The county gave preliminary approval to build 10 homes. The builder closed in 1988 paying $425,000 for the property. He did not get owner's title insurance.

When the builder applied for final site plan approval, the county discovered that the land had been proffered to the school board in 1974 for a school site. The county now refuses to approve the site plan and demands conveyance to the school board. The builder may lose the project and still owe his banks $350,000 borrowed to buy the land.

THE BUYER'S RECOURSE If someone makes a claim against the title after closing, the buyer has recourse against the seller and perhaps the title examiner. If the seller provides a general warranty deed, in Virginia, he guarantees title all the way back to the King of England. The seller would be responsible for all defects. If you cannot find the seller, or he is not financially capable of paying, this guarantee is of little value to the buyer. Even if the seller is available, the buyer must pay attorney fees and costs associated with defending his title and recovering from the seller. The seller is not responsible for those costs.

If the defect was a matter of record, the title examiner might be liable. You must prove that a normally prudent title examiner practicing in the area would have discovered the defect. This involves more expensive litigation. If the matter was not of record, the title examiner would have no liability. In all three cases above, the title examiner would not be liable.

In a title related lawsuit each owner sues his seller. This could involve you even after you have sold the property. Ideally, the suit reaches back to the person who caused the claim. More often, someone is unable to find their seller or the wrongdoer is insolvent. Like a game a musical chairs, the last one who can't find a defendant is the loser.

If the owner has a title insurance policy, these issues are of no concern. The title insurance company would defend against the claim or resolve the matter. The company pays all costs, including attorney fees, in defense of these claims.

ADDITIONAL BENEFITS Owner's title insurance has an additional benefit when selling. If a defect, or even a question, arises, there must be a remedy before you can sell the property. Delays result while the uninsured seller tries to clear title. Under many contracts, the seller has sixty days to clear title or the buyer can declare him in default. Then the seller is liable to the buyer for damages, as well as owing the person claiming against his property! If the seller has title insurance, many times the insurance company can insure over the problem without postponing the closing. The insurance company clears the matter up later.

Coverage for Lenders and Owners Lender's coverage protects the lender's interest in the property. As the loan pays down, the coverage also decreases. If a claim arises after payoff of the loan, there is no coverage.

Owner's coverage protects the buyer's interest in the property. It continues to protect the owner even after he sells the property. Most owner's policies also contain an inflation endorsement. These automatically increase coverage each year (up to 125% of the sale price). As the loan balance pays down and the value increases, owner's coverage protects the growing equity. Without an owner's policy, any loss comes out of the owner's pocket. The lender's policy does not cover the claim unless it is so large it threatens the loan.

ISSUING THE POLICY   The chain of paperwork to issue a policy includes:

1) Title Abstract - This is the accumulation of a title examiner's notes from the courthouse records. The abstract is data in its raw form. The title examiner renders no opinions. The abstract includes a summary of all documents which might effect title to the property including deeds, deeds of trust, covenants and conditions, easements, certificates of satisfaction, judgments etc.

2) Title Binder - Based on information in the abstract, the title binder represents the insurance company's written commitment to insure title. It is subject to certain exceptions and conditions based on an analysis of the abstract. Exceptions are matters the title insurance company will not insure against. Examples are existing easements and covenants, or mislocated fences.

The company may chose to provide limited coverage to the lender or owner. Limited coverage insures against loss or damage. It means the insured must suffer an actual out of pocket loss as a result of a claim. More complete coverage insures marketability. It protects if a later buyer refuses to go forward with a purchase because of concern over the defect, even though no one has yet made a claim.

Conditions are requirements to satisfy. These include releasing liens, correcting errors in previous documents, locating heirs or providing proof of death in estate cases.

3) Title Insurance Policy - The policy itself is issued after settlement and recording of the documents.

WHEN TITLE INSURANCE DOESN'T WORK

Title insurance companies are in the unique position of being able to exclude certain risks from coverage. It would be like a fire insurance policy that said, since you live in an area that is dry in the summer, we won't cover you against brush fires.

A title insurance company can take exception to a potential title defect. It might give limited coverage against the defect, agreeing to insure only if there is an actual claim but not covering marketability. That means, if a future buyer objects to the defect, you have no coverage unless potential problem has resulted in an actual claim.

The title insurance company might give coverage to your lender, but not include coverage for you as the owner. An example might be coverage against mechanic's liens filed by unpaid contractors or matters disclosed on a survey. These are often included in lender's policies but not owner's. The insidious part of all this is most buyers never see the title insurance binder and don't understand they are not getting full coverage.

How do you protect yourself? First, if an attorney is not conducting the closing, have an attorney review the package. Ask to see the title binder. Be especially careful when the title will be issued by someone who has another interest in the transaction. If the real estate company or lender has an interest in the title agency, you may find your best interest being subordinated to theirs.

Consider getting an enhanced coverage policy such as the First American Title Insurance Company's EAGLE POLICY. It contains coverage against survey errors, building code violations, and post policy matters such as identity theft and forgery. First American has an excellent website at TitleCentral.com.

TAX ISSUES

HOW TO HANDLE INTEREST DEDUCTIONS

The deduction for home mortgage interest and real estate taxes is one of the last shelters left in our tax laws. However, the laws are complicated. Different rules apply to the interest deduction depending upon when you purchased or refinanced the home. Special rules apply to acquisition loans, home equity loans and loans for home improvements. The discussion here is general. You must consult with a tax advisor for specific advice for your particular situation.

THE INTEREST DEDUCTION Home mortgage interest is deductible, with certain limitations, when either a primary and second home secures the loan.

The payment must be for your loan. Interest is only deductible by the person obligated to pay it to the lender. If you did not sign the loan documents, you were not obligated on the loan. If you pay a mortgage for someone else, such as a family member or joint owner, then the interest is not deductible. Furthermore, since the person obligated did not actually make the payment, he can not deduct the interest either. That is also why points paid by a seller are not deductible against his income. They are not charges on his loan. However, they are a cost of sale and reduce his gain on the sale.

THE SECOND HOME You can claim an interest deduction on two homes. "Home" is broadly defined and includes anything that contains sleeping space, toilet and cooking facilities. Houses, condominiums, and cooperatives, all clearly qualify. Boats, motor homes, and house trailers also qualify if they meet the criteria.

If you rent the second home during the tax year, you must use it for personal purposes at least 14 days during the year or 10% of the total number of days you rent, whichever is greater. If you use it less, the second home is investment property and the passive loss limitations associated with investment property apply.

LIMITATIONS ON DEDUCTIBILITY Three factors limit the interest deduction: when you closed the loan, the amount of the loan, and the use of the proceeds. If the total interest exceeds the allowable amount, or fails to qualify for some other reason, then the difference is personal interest. Beginning in 1991, none of it is deductible. Any personal interest that cannot be deducted is added to the basis of the property and reduces the tax due on sale.

LOANS CLOSED BEFORE OCTOBER 13, 1987 The interest deduction was generally unlimited before this date. Home mortgage interest on any number of homes was deductible.

If you refinance one of these loans later, the old balance is under the old rules. If the new balance exceeds the old, then the increased amount is subject to the new rules.

If the loan was a line of credit then the old rules govern the outstanding balance on October 13, 1987. Any money advanced after that date is subject to the new rules. A line of credit loan allows a borrower a certain amount of credit. He can borrow and repay and re-borrow up to the amount of the line. The total indebtedness outstanding at any one time can not exceed the agreed amount. Many home equity loans are lines of credit.

LOANS CLOSED AFTER OCTOBER 13, 1987 After this date, only two homes may qualify as personal residences. The use of the proceeds also becomes a determining factor. Proceeds are either acquisition indebtedness or home equity indebtedness.

Acquisition indebtedness is money to buy, build, or substantially improve a first or second home. Acquisition debt is a misleading term. You do not need to place the loan when you buy the property. If the loan is for improvements, it is acquisition debt even though the loan and improvements are done after you acquire the home. Thus, a home improvement loan would become part of the acquisition debt.

You may deduct interest on a total of $1,000,000 dollars of acquisition debt. Add all mortgages including ones before October 13, 1987 as they are part of the $1,000,000 dollar limit.

If you refinance a loan, the outstanding balance of the acquisition debt continues as acquisition debt. Any additional borrowing, not used for home improvements, is home equity indebtedness, discussed below.

For home equity debt, the limit is $100,000 of principle. Any interest charged on loan balances above $100,000 is personal interest. If the funds were not to buy, build or substantially improve a first or second home, the loan is a home equity loan. Interest charged on balances above the $100,000 limit is personal interest.

If a loan is for more than one purpose, then it is a mixed-use mortgage. Allocate the proceeds between home equity and acquisition debt depending on the use of funds. Then divide the total interest charge between the categories. So long as the acquisition portion remains below $1,000,000 and the home equity portion below $100,000, all of the interest is deductible. If you exceed one of the limits, the proportionate share of interest is personal interest.

POINTS Loan fees or points are a form of prepaid interest. Prepaid interest is not deductible in the year paid. You must amortize or spread it over the life of the loan. For a thirty year loan, deduct one-thirtieth of the points each year. Claim any remaining undeducted points in the year you pay off the loan.

There is an exception for points on loans secured by your main home and used to buy or improve your main home. If the buyer meets these requirements, all points (including those paid by the seller) are deductible, by the buyer, in the year paid. Only amounts usually charged by lenders in the area qualify.

You must amortize points for a loan on your second home or investment property. If you place a loan on your main home and use it to buy an investment property, you must amortize the points. Likewise, if you place a loan on investment property but use it to improve your home, amortize the points.

To qualify for the immediate write-off, the charge must be for prepaid interest. Discount points clearly qualify when paid by the borrower. Do not deduct charges for specific services such as placing, insuring or servicing the loan. VA funding fees, FHA insurance premiums, underwriting fees, document preparation fees, appraisal fees etc. are not interest. They are part of the expense of buying the house.

Add non-interest charges to the cost or basis of the house. You receive no immediate write-off. However, since the basis increases, this reduces the tax owed or rolled over when you sell the house.

LOAN ORIGINATION FEES There has been a battle over whether origination fees are for interest or servicing. The latest rulings indicate they are deductible in the year of purchase of an owner-occupied home.

POINTS ON REFINANCES You must amortize points paid to refinance a loan. The exception is that portion of the loan used for home improvements. Amortize points on the old loan balance. Deduct the points on the additional financing used for improvements.

HOME EQUITY LOAN POINTS Deduct points charged on that portion of a home equity loan used for improvements. If you use the home equity loan for other purposes, amortize the points not attributable to the home improvements portion of the loan.

HOW TO HANDLE MOVING EXPENSE DEDUCTIONS

If you move in connection with your work, you may deduct the costs of the move. This includes travel and house hunting expenses, meals, lodging and other costs. There are limitations on the type and amount of expenses and you must itemize deductions to qualify. The deduction is available to both employees and self-employed individuals. Cross town moves are generally not covered but the deduction is available for moves both within and outside the United States.

The discussion here is general and we strongly recommend that you consult with a tax advisor for specific advice for your particular situation.

WHO CLAIMS THE DEDUCTION? You must be gainfully employed or self-employed to qualify. A semi-retired person or a part timer who only works a few hours a week cannot claim the deduction. You may include household member's expenses.

COMMENCING WORK Your move must be work related. It should be close, both in time and place, to the start of work at your new job location. It is not necessary to have a contract or commitment of employment before moving so long as you actually do go to work. You can take a new job or a first job or your employer may move your job to a new location. You must make your move within one year or show special circumstances that prevented you from moving within one year. For example, if you delay your move so your children can finish high school in the same school, that is a sufficient reason.

THE DISTANCE REQUIREMENT Your new principal place of work must be at least 35 miles farther from your old residence than your old place of work was from your old residence. For example, if the distance from home to work is now 5 miles, the distance from your new job to your old home must be at least 40 miles. Use the shortest of commonly traveled routes, not "as the crow flies." If a couple file a joint return and both of them work, only one of them needs to meet the distance requirement. If your new residence is farther from work than your old residence was, you must show that there is an actual decrease in commuting time.

THE PRINCIPAL PLACE OF WORK If you work in several locations or for several employers, your principal place of work where you spend the greater part of your working time, or where you earn the most money.

THE REQUIRED EMPLOYMENT PERIOD Provided you meet the distance test, you must actually work for a certain time at the new location. The required period is different depending upon whether you are employed or self-employed.

EMPLOYED PERSONS If you are an employee, you must work full time in the general location of your new residence. You must work at least 39 weeks in the 12 month period after you arrive in the new location. The 39 week test is waived only in the event of death, disability, involuntary separation (but not for misconduct) or transfer for the benefit of your employer. If you file a joint return, only one spouse need meet the requirements.

SELF EMPLOYED PERSONS Self-employed persons must work at least 78 weeks in the 24 month period following arrival at the new place of work. In addition, you must work at least 39 weeks in the first year. If you become self-employed you can include the time you were working as an employee.

WHEN TO CLAIM THE DEDUCTION Often you will not have satisfied the time tests when your tax return is due. Deduct the expenses in the year they were incurred or in the year you received a taxable reimbursement from your employer. You may choose to take the deduction even though you have not yet fulfilled the requirements or wait and file an amended return. If you claim the deduction and then do not meet the time period requirements, you will owe tax. You can either file an amended return and pay tax on the improperly deducted amount or include the amount in your gross income the following year.

DEDUCTIBLE MOVING EXPENSES You can only deduct reasonable, not extravagant, moving expenses. These include the following:

      Travel during the move including the cost of meals and lodging,
      Moving of household goods,
      Travel on house hunting trips after finding employment,
      Meals and lodging in temporary quarters,
      Costs connected with the purchase, sale or lease of a residence.

TRAVEL DURING THE MOVE You can deduct 80% of the cost of meals and the entire amount of transportation and lodging. You may only make one trip but if individual family members travel separately, those trips are deductible.

MOVING HOUSEHOLD GOODS Deduct the cost of moving vans, packing, and shipping. Deduct storage and insurance costs if they are incurred within 30 days of the move.

TRAVEL WHILE HOUSE HUNTING You must already be employed, and the principal purpose of the trip must be house hunting. If you are self employed, you only need to have made substantial arrangements to start work. The cost of your return trip is also deductible. The trip does not have to be successful. You may take any number of trips. Only deduct 80% of the cost of meals.

MEALS AND LODGING IN TEMPORARY QUARTERS Deduct reasonable expenses incurred within any one period of 30 consecutive days. Only deduct 80% of the cost of meals and do not deduct any personal expenses such as entertainment or laundry. The temporary quarters must be in the general location of your new work and are not deductible if you temporarily rent where you used to work. Also you may not deduct rent on a pre-occupancy agreement while you wait to buy the same house. You must have a job or if self-employed, have made substantial arrangements to start work.

SALE, PURCHASE OR LEASE EXPENSES   Sale and purchase expenses are normally items deducted from the taxable profit when you sell your house. When you incur the expenses in connection with a qualified move, they can be deducted immediately. These include: attorney fees, real estate commissions, points, transfer taxes and recording fees, and expenses reasonably necessary to make the sale. Do not include fix up expenses. Lease expenses include amounts paid to have your lease canceled. They do not include forfeitures of a security deposit or rent for breaking a lease. A loss incurred in the sale of a personal residence is not deductible.

DOLLAR LIMITATIONS   You may not deduct more than $3,000 total for house hunting trips, temporary living expenses, and sale purchase and lease expenses. The amount for house hunting and temporary quarters may not exceed $1,500. Apply any purchase expenses that you cannot deduct because of these limits to increase the basis in the new home. Excess sale expenses would decrease the gain on the old home.

MEMBERS OF THE ARMED FORCES   If you are on active duty, you do not need to meet the distance and time test if the move is in connection with a permanent change of station. This includes a move from your home to your first duty post, a move from your last duty post to your home, and a move from one permanent duty post to another.

MOVES TO AND FROM FOREIGN COUNTRIES   In general these moves are subject to the same time, distance and reasonableness requirements. However, the dollar limitations are higher. You can deduct up to 90 days of temporary living expenses. You can deduct the costs of moving your personal effects to and from storage and storing them for all or part of the time you job remains outside of the United States. Retirees who move back from a foreign country may take moving expenses even though the move is not in connection with starting a new job. A similar rule allows the deduction for survivors of a deceased worker who move back within six months of the date of death.

HOW TO DEFER GAIN ON THE SALE OF A PERSONAL RESIDENCE AND TAX DEFERRED EXCHANGES OF INVESTMENT PROPERTY

You must pay tax when you sell property for a profit but liberal rules allow an exclusion of gain when you sell a personal residence. Sadly, there is no provision to take a tax loss on the sale of a personal residence. Different, rules apply to investment property.

SALE OF PERSONAL RESIDENCE

IRS Publication 523, "Tax Information on Selling Your Home" is available free from local IRS offices. To order mail, call 1-800-TAX-FORM (1-800-829-3676).

For sales after May 6, 1997, anyone can completely exclude up to $500,000 of gain on a joint return ($250,000 if filing singly).

What are the Limits? You must own and occupy the sold property as your personal residence for at least two of the five years preceding the sale. The two years do not need to be continuous so long as the total periods aggregate two years or more. You could occupy for six months each year for four years to total your two years of occupancy.

You can only use the exclusion once every two years.

Partial Exclusions The new law recognizes a partial exclusion if you fail to meet the two year use and ownership requirement or if you must sell more than once in two years. For instance, if you only used the property as your personal residence for one year instead of two, you could exclude half the amount of gain. The partial exclusion is only available if you sold due to change in your place of employment, health or to the "extent provided in regulations, unforeseen circumstances. Consult a tax advisor if you rented the property as you may have to recapture depreciation.

SALE OF INVESTMENT PROPERTY

Tax on investment property sales can be deferred through use of a tax –deferred exchange. Why is deferral important? There is an obvious advantage to postponing payment of taxes. The time value of money and inflation means a bill paid in the future does not cost as much as a bill paid today. If you retire and sell the property, you will be in a lower tax bracket. If you die, the property passes to your heirs at the market value at the time of your death. An entire lifetime of gain goes untaxed.

A less obvious, but equally compelling, advantage is the effect of leverage. Consider the sale of a property having a taxable profit of $100,000. Combined state and federal taxes of 38% would leave only $62,000 available to re-invest. If that $62,000 were a 20% down payment, you could purchase new property worth $340,000. If you had the entire $100,000 to put down, you could buy $500,000 of new property. If the property appreciates 5% a year, you earn $17,000 per year on one bought after paying taxes and $25,000 on the other.

An investor may want to defer tax because he will not realize sufficient cash from the sale transaction. The investor may have refinanced and not have enough equity to pay the tax owed.

In addition, investors take tax write-offs in the form of depreciation. Depreciation saves money on today's taxes but reduces the owner's basis in the property. Basis is the term used to describe where you start to calculate taxable profit. The seller owes tax on the difference between the reduced basis and the sale price. Using a tax deferred exchange allows the investor to postpone paying.

Section 1031 of the Internal Revenue Code provides, in part, "No gain or loss shall be recognized on the exchange of property held for productive use in a trade or business, or for investment, if such property is exchanged solely for property of a like-kind which is to be held either for productive use in a trade or business or for investment."

If anything of value, other than like-kind property, is thrown in "to boot" you pay tax on the amount of the "boot."

Originally, the exchange requirement meant you had to find an investor who owned a property you wanted or who would buy one you wanted and swap with him in a simultaneous exchange. Mr. Starker stretched this rule by selling his property and putting the funds in escrow. He then bought new property with the escrowed funds, in a delayed rather than direct simultaneous exchange. The IRS objected but the Courts held for Mr. Starker giving rise to the so-called Starker or delayed exchange. After years of fighting the issue, the IRS has issued regulations for a delayed exchange.

With a delayed exchange, the investor may close on the sale of his property before he has settled on, or even identified the target or replacement property. He must identify the new replacement property, in writing, within 45 days of the first closing. He may designate up to three potential replacement properties. He can even designate more than three but the total value may not exceed 200% of the sale price of the old property. If he exceeds both the three-property and the 200% rules, the exchange is valid only if he acquires property that is at least 95% of the fair market value of all the property identified.

If he designates a property and changes his mind, he can revoke the designation and select other property if he is still within the 45 days. Slip up and miss the date, or designate too much property and you lose the tax deferred exchange.

The seller must consummate the exchange by closing on the new property no later than 180 days after the first closing or before his tax return for the year is filed. Shorter allowable times between transactions are the second distinction between investment and personal residence rollover.

The third distinction is the handling of the proceeds of sale. The seller cannot have access to the money during the 45/180 day time frame. An independent escrow agent, known as a qualified intermediary, holds the funds and uses them to buy the replacement property for the exchanger.

ADJUSTING BASIS   With an exchange, tax is not forgiven, only deferred. The basis in property sold transfers to the new property. If you buy a property for $100,000 and sell it for $150,000, replacing it with one costing $150,000, the new property has a $100,000 basis. When you sell it later for $250,000, the taxable profit is $150,000.

If you buy a new property adding money, those additional funds add to the basis. So, if you sold for $150,000 and bought a new property for $170,000, the additional $20,000 would raise your basis to $120,000. When you sell later for $250,000, the taxable profit is $130,000.

If you had depreciated the old property $10,000, your basis in the old property would be $90,000. Your gain on the first sale would be $60,000. If exchanged, there would be no tax owed on this profit but the basis in the second property would be $90,000. Following the example a step further, the final sale at $250,000 would generate a $160,000 taxable profit.

QUALIFYING PROPERTY   Exchanged property must be like-kind. Fortunately, regulations define the term liberally. Any real estate, whether or not it is improved, qualifies as like-kind. You can exchange a house in Florida for a farm in Virginia and a condominium in Hawaii. You can sell one property and buy two or more.

You cannot sell a business and buy real estate, unless you price the real estate and business separately.

Any property that is not like-kind is treated as boot and you must pay tax on the boot. The most common form of boot is cash. If you swap property and end up with cash left over, you have received boot and pay tax on the cash. If you receive property with a loan lower than the loan you gave up, you have received boot in the form of mortgage relief - add cash from outside the transaction to avoid boot. The replacement property should have mortgage debt or new cash added, equal to or greater than the mortgage debt of the old property.

A simple rule is: 1) buy up - get a more expensive property, 2) borrow up - with at least as big a loan, and 3) use up - use all of the equity so you have no cash left over. If necessary, pay down the loan on the new property.

THE QUALIFIED INTERMEDIARY Delayed exchanges are much more common than simultaneous. After the first sale closes, a qualified intermediary holds the sale proceeds in escrow. The intermediary is sometimes called an accommodator or facilitator and must be independent of the parties. (Don't use your brother - in - law). Our firm can supply you with the qualified intermediary.

The intermediary establishes the escrow account and acts for the purchaser and seller/exchanger arranging for the transfer of funds and deeding the property. Obviously you will want to check out the intermediary carefully. Are they bonded or insured? Be sure your funds are held in a separately identified trust account.

The intermediary also receives the 45 day notice designating the replacement property.

The seller has no access to the funds during the 45/180 day period except to purchase the exchange property. He may direct the intermediary to use funds for the deposit, but not for improvements. Interest earned belongs to the seller but it is taxable.

HOW DO YOU DO IT? You should recognize the need for a tax deferred exchange if the seller:

1) has investment property,
2) intends to buy new investment property and
3) will be subject to tax liability on the sale.

The tax aspects of a deferred exchange are complicated. Speak with a tax expert. The expert can assist with issues such as adjusted basis and the appropriate price and financing for the replacement or target property.

CONTRACT LANGUAGE There should be language in the listing and in the sale and purchase contracts to make it obvious the investor intends to accomplish a tax deferred exchange.

Here are the three suggested paragraphs to include:

TAX DEFERRED EXCHANGE LISTING [92]

The owner intends to accomplish a tax deferred exchange. Any contract should provide for Purchaser cooperation. Contact lister for details.

TAX DEFERRED EXCHANGE SALES CONTRACT [93]

This transaction will be a Section 1031 Tax Deferred Exchange at no additional expense or liability to the Purchaser. The intention of the Parties is for the Seller/Exchanger to use Section 1031 of the Internal Revenue Code to postpone taxes by exchanging this Property for other property (insert description or "to be designated later and acquired through a trust established at settlement"). The Purchaser and Seller/Exchanger will execute necessary documents to complete the exchange, including any assignments or trust agreements.

The Seller will pay all expenses associated with the tax deferred exchange and hold the Purchaser harmless from any liability in connection therewith. All references to "Seller" in the Contract shall mean Seller/Exchanger.

TAX DEFERRED EXCHANGE PURCHASE CONTRACT [94]

This transaction will be a Section 1031 Tax Deferred Exchange at no additional expense or liability to the Seller. The intention of the parties is for the Purchaser/Exchanger to use Section 1031 of the Internal Revenue Code to postpone taxes by receiving this Property through a delayed exchange for other property. Purchaser/Exchanger will place funds in escrow to complete the exchange. The Seller and Purchaser/Exchanger will execute necessary documents to complete the exchange including any assignments or trust agreements.

The Purchaser will pay all expenses associated with the tax deferred exchange and hold the Seller harmless from any liability in connection therewith.

All references to "Purchaser" in the Contract shall mean Purchaser/Exchanger.

WHY RENTAL REAL ESTATE IS AN "IDEAL" INVESTMENT

The use of the word "IDEAL" provides a convenient mnemonic device.

Rental real estate is the IDEAL investment because it provides Income, Depreciation, Equity, Appreciation and Leverage:

Income - rental property provides rental income to the investor

Depreciation - allows you to write off a part of the value of the property each year thus reducing taxes on other income

Equity - each rental payment, applied to a mortgage reduced the mortgage balance and increases the equity in the property. Even if the rent is just equal to the mortgage payment, over time the tenant pays for the property.

Appreciation - over long periods, real estate gains value.

Leverage - A relatively small down-payment is combined with a loan. If you have $10,000 invested in a $100,000 home and it goes up in value by $10,000, you have doubled your money even though the investment only appreciated by 10%.

SECTION FOUR - FORMS

CONTRACT FOR DEED ADDENDUM

The parties to the Sales Contract dated _____ , 20_____
between

_____

(Purchasers) and

_____

Sellers) for the property located at:

_____

hereby agree as follows:

1) The Seller financing referenced in the Sales Contract shall be an installment sale using a Contract for Deed. The parties will execute, acknowledge and deliver the Contract for Deed and Escrow Agreement, Note, Deed and Release of Contract as well as Disclosure and other documents at settlement.

2) Title will remain in the name of the seller. Purchaser will have a contract interest in the Property. Title will not pass to the Purchaser until the Purchaser either: a) pays the existing loan in full, or b) formally assumes the existing loan. Purchaser will make payments _____ directly to the lender or _____ to the Seller who shall pay the lender or _____ to a third party who shall pay the lender.

3) All existing mortgages remain in the Seller's name and Seller remains liable for the mortgage payments. Purchaser _____ may or _____ may not take over Seller's loan by means of a qualifying assumption without a release of Seller or Seller's VA eligibility (if applicable).

4) If Purchaser defaults on the Contract for Deed obligations, Purchaser may lose the property and all sums paid including downpayment, mortgage payments, home improvements shall be deemed occupancy changes and any equity in the property shall revert to Seller. The Seller may need to pay existing mortgage payments, real estate and insurance costs, and costs to re-market and sell the property in order to protect the Seller's interest.

5) All costs incurred by Seller (including those above) as a result of Purchaser's default shall become an additional personal debt of the Purchaser subject to collection procedures by Seller including a lawsuit judgment, and garnishment of wages and other assets.

6) This transaction may violate the due-on-sale clause in the existing mortgage. This means the lender may call the loan immediately due and payable. If the Purchaser is unable to refinance or qualify for an assumption, foreclosure may result.

7) There is no guarantee that the Purchaser will ever be able to assume or refinance the existing mortgage(s). The ability of the Purchaser to consummate the obligations under the Contract for Deed will depend on the Purchaser's credit worthiness and the market which dictates property values and loan rates.

8) The parties are not relying on any representations from the real estate agents or brokers concerning the Purchasers future ability to consummate the obligations under the Contract for Deed. The parties acknowledge they have been advised to seek the advice of an attorney of their own choosing concerning this transaction.

9) The parties remove any contingencies regarding advice from counsel and desire to proceed to closing. The costs of preparing the Contract for Deed and related documents will be divided equally.

SEEN AND AGREED to this _____ day of _____,
20_____.

_____
PURCHASER   SELLER

_____
PURCHASER   SELLER

DEED OF TRUST NOTE (Virginia)

$, Virginia   , 20

FOR VALUE RECEIVED, the undersigned (jointly and severally, of more than one) promise to pay to the order of   at such place as the holder hereof may designate, the principal sum of   Dollars ($), together with interest thereon at the rate of   percent (%) per annum from the date hereof until paid.

Payments on the principal sum and the interest thereon shall be payable in monthly installments of   ($) each on the   day of each and every month commencing   , 19   , and continuing until   ,   , when the remaining unpaid balance of this indebtedness, and interest thereon, shall be due and payable. Each monthly installment paid hereunder shall be applied first to interest then due on the unpaid principal and the remainder if any shall be applied to the unpaid balance of this indebtedness.

The makers have the privilege at any time of prepaying all or part of the principal balance and interest remaining due and unpaid without penalty or premium of any kind.

It is expressly agreed that upon failure of the undersigned to perform or comply with any of the terms and conditions hereof of any of the covenants and conditions contained in this Note, then and in any or all such events, the holder hereof shall have the right to declare the entire unpaid balance of this indebtedness, together with all accrued interest, charges, expenses, advances and attorney's fees, and failure to exercise such right shall not constitute a waiver of the right to exercise the same upon any subsequent failure.

We, the undersigned, and any guarantors or endorsers hereof, jointly and severally, waive the benefit of our Homestead exemption as to this obligation, and hereby waive notice of presentment, protect, demand and notice of dishonor, and notice of and consent to any extensions of this Note; and further agree to pay reasonable attorney's fees should it become necessary to place this Note in the hands of an attorney for collection or to protect the interest of the holder hereof as provided in the Deed of Trust securing this Note.

The maker of this Note shall pay the Noteholder a late charge of   percent (%) of each payment more than   (   ) days in arrears.

In the event the property secured hereby is sold, or title is otherwise transferred except by death, the entire indebtedness hereby secured shall become due and payable, at the option of the holder of this Note. In the event the lender elects to allow this loan to be assumed, it shall not relieve the maker of the Note from liability.

WITNESS THE FOLLOWING SIGNATURE(S) AND SEAL(S):

_____(SEAL)

_____(SEAL)

P.O. Address:

   This is to certify that this is the promissory Note described in a certain Deed of Trust of even date herewith, to   and   , Trustees, the said Deed of Trust having been signed in my presence.

My Commission Expires:

_____
NOTARY PUBLIC

(When this Note has been paid, you must obtain and record a Certificate of Satisfaction or Deed of Release to release the Deed of Trust from the land records.)

DEED OF TRUST (Virginia)

THIS DEED OF TRUST, made and entered into this　　day of　　, 20　　, by and between

　　　　　("Grantor"), and　　　　　of　　　　　County, Virginia; and of　　　　　County , Virginia ("Trustees");

W I T N E S S E T H :

That for and in consideration of the sum of TEN DOLLARS ($10.00), the said Grantor grants,

bargains, sells and conveys unto the said Trustee(s), WITH GENERAL WARRANTY OF TITLE, certain

real estate in the　　of　　, State of Virginia, more particularly described as follows:

NOTICE: THE DEBT SECURED HEREBY IS SUBJECT TO CALL IN FULL OR THE TERMS THEREOF BEING MODIFIED IN THE EVENT OF SALE OR CONVEYANCE OF THE PROPERTY CONVEYED.

Also including (but not excluding any fixtures which would ordinarily be construed as a part of the realty) any and all storm sashes, storm doors, vestibules, wire screens, wire doors, window shades, awnings, trees, shrubs, oil burner or other furnace equipment, domestic hot water boiler and equipment, and refrigerators, stoves and appliances now installed, used in the building upon said premises at the time of the execution of this Deed of Trust, including, as well, all apparatus and fixtures of every description for watering, heating, ventilating, air conditioning, and screening said premises, together with all and singular the improvements, ways, easements, rights, privileges, and appurtenances to the same belonging, or in anywise appertaining.

As further security for the debt hereby secured and the interest thereon and all of the sums authorized to be expended by the Trustees or the Noteholder, the Grantor hereby also sell, transfer and assign unto the Noteholder, prior and superior to any and all other claims or demands thereto, the rents, issues, and income of and from the above described property accrued and hereafter to accrue, with full power and authority, at the Noteholder's election, to collect and give receipts in full for the same and to apply all sums so collected. There shall be no duty upon the said Noteholder, however, to exercise such election and the Noteholder may permit the Grantor at any time and from time to time to collect said rents, issues, and income to their own use in which event the same shall in no way be deemed a waiver by, or to work an estoppel upon , the said Noteholder thereafter to assert such holder's full rights and authority hereunder, provided, further, that no prepaying of any said rents, issues, or income for the whole or any portion of the said property, shall be procured, or permitted, or valid without the written consent of the Noteholder. If, moreover, upon default in the payment of any amount secured by this Deed of Trust, the Grantor or its successors in title to the property herein conveyed shall be or remain in possession thereof, or any part thereof, they shall do so as tenants at will and they shall be obligated to pay to the Noteholder a fair and reasonable rental for the premises so occupied so long as they remain, or are allowed to remain, in such possession.

IN TRUST, HOWEVER, to secure the prompt payment of   certain negotiable

promissory note   bearing even date herein, as follows:

AMOUNT:

MADE BY:

AND PAYABLE TO THE ORDER OF:

after date, at such place as the holder may designate, or at such other place as the holder of the note may

designate from time to time in writing, without offset, with interest at the rate of percent

(%) per annum until paid, providing for monthly installments to interest and principal,

with the balance of the indebtedness, if not sooner paid, due and payable on

,   .

ADDITIONAL TERMS:

Said Note waives the homestead exemption as to the Makers and Endorsers thereof; and waives notice of maturity, presentment, demand, protest and notice of protest, notice of non-payment and dishonor of the Note, and has been identified by the Notary Public before whom these presents are acknowledged.

The maker of this Note shall pay the Noteholder a late charge of $.05 for each $1.00 of each payment more than _____ days in arrears.

The privilege is reserved to pay the unpaid principal balance in full at any time, without penalty.

In case the Note is collected through an attorney-at-law, or under the advice thereof, the undersigned agree to pay all costs of collection, including reasonable attorney fees.

Also, in Trust, to secure the payment of any renewals or extensions of said debt and when the same shall become due and payable, and of all costs and expenses incurred in respect thereto, and of all costs and expenses, including reasonable counsel fees incurred or paid by the Trustees, or by any party hereby secured, on account of any litigation at law or in equity which may arise in respect to this Deed of Trust, and of all moneys which may be advanced as herein provided, with interest at the rate of 15.0% per annum on all such costs and sums so advanced from the date of such advance; and also in trust to secure the performance of all the covenants on the party of the grantors herein covenanted to be performed.

Except as herein otherwise provided, this Deed of Trust shall be construed in accordance with the provisions of the Code of Virginia, as amended.

Provided that the Trustees shall not be required to see that this Deed of Trust is recorded and shall not be liable for the default or misconduct of any agent or attorney appointed by them in pursuance hereof, or for anything whatever in connection with this trust, including actions taken while the Trustees are in possession of the property pursuant to the default provisions of this agreement except willful misconduct or gross negligence. Trustees may act upon any instrument believed by them in good faith to be genuine and signed by the proper party or parties, and shall be fully protected for any action taken by them in reliance thereon.

Should one of the Trustees herein named die or decline or fail to execute this trust, then the other Trustee shall have all the rights, powers and authority, and be charged with all the duties that are hereby conferred or charged upon both, unless and until a Co-Trustee be appointed.

The said Grantor covenants: to pay the indebtedness hereby secured as and when the same shall become due and payable; to pay all taxes and assessments on said premises when due and immediately thereafter exhibit the official receipts to the holder of the said Note; to keep the improvements now on said property or any that may hereafter be erected thereon insured, for such coverage, in an amount equal to the replacement costs of the improvements now thereon or the outstanding amount of the indebtedness, whichever is less, and to assign the same with loss payable to the Noteholder, and any amount received from said insurance shall be applied in reduction or payment of the debt hereby secured to the repair or rebuilding of the improvements, at the option of the Grantor; to pay promptly any and all sums which have or may at any time hereafter become due for labor and materials furnished in or about the construction of any improvements on said land, and to satisfy forthwith any indebtedness for which a notice of intention to claim Mechanics' or Materialmen's Liens may at any time be filed against said land and premises; not to do nor suffer to be done anything to depreciate or impair the value of the said property; and upon default or neglect in the performance of any said covenants the holder of said Note may pay such taxes and assessments, and have the said improvements insured, and pay and satisfy any debt for labor and materials furnished in, on or about the said premises, and take steps to prevent depreciation or impairment of the value of the said property, and all expenses thereof shall be secured hereby, repayable upon demand, and shall bear interest at the rate of 15% per annum from the date of any such payment or payments.

At the Noteholder's option and provided no senior Noteholder is collecting escrows for taxes and insurance, the Grantor agrees to make an additional payment to the Noteholder monthly during the time that the indebtedness remains unpaid, of an amount equal to one-twelfth of annual taxes and assessments and/or premiums on insurance on the property on which the Note is secured or any other insurance policies, the premium for which are to be paid by the Noteholder.

Any default in the payment of any lien or encumbrances senior hereto shall give the holder of the Note secured hereby the option to call said Note for payment in full regardless of the payment status of the Note secured hereby or, in the sole discretion of the holder of the Note secured hereby, it may cure the default and add the cost and expenses of curing same to the amount due under this Deed of Trust and Note secured hereby.

The following phrases are to be interpreted in accord with Virginia Code Section 55-60:

Exemptions waived. Right of anticipation reserved. Subject to all upon default. Substitution of Trustee permitted. Renewal or extension permitted. Any Trustee may act. Reinstatement permitted.

In the event of default in the payment of said Note or any installment of principal or interest as and when the same shall become due and payable, or upon default in any respect to any of the covenants herein contained, the Trustees, here named, or the Trustee or Trustees acting in the execution of this Trust shall, upon being requested by the holder of the Note hereby secured, sell the property hereby conveyed at public auction for cash upon the premises, or at the front door of the Court House of the County or City wherein the said property is located, or at some other place in the said County or City selected by the Trustees (and a bidder's deposit of as much as 10% of the principal then due on the Note may be required), after advertising the time, terms and place of sale in at least two weekly issues of some newspaper either published of having a general circulation the said County or City, at the discretion of the Trustees, and shall convey the same to, and at the cost of, the purchaser thereof, who shall not be required to see to the application of the purchase money, and from the proceeds of said sale, shall pay, FIRST, all proper cost, charges, and expenses, including a Trustees' commission of 5% of the gross amount of sale, or the sum of $500.00, whichever is greater, in addition to reasonable fees to counsel for the trustees in conducting such sale or expended by the Noteholder in collection efforts prior to the sale, of not less than $500.00; SECOND, all taxes, levies and assessments, with costs and interest, against the same property hereby conveyed due on date of sale; THIRD, the total amount of principal, including any advances thereon, unpaid on said indebtedness, with interest to date, whether the same be due or not; and the balance, if any, shall be paid to the owner of the said property hereby conveyed at the time of said sale upon delivery of possession of the said property hereby conveyed, less the cost, if any, in obtaining possession thereof; provided, however, that the Trustee or Trustees, as to such residue, shall not be bound by any inheritance, devise, conveyance, assignment of lien of or upon the grantor's equity, without actual notice thereof prior to distribution.

And it is further covenanted and agreed that if the said property shall be advertised for sale as herein provided, and not sold, the Trustee or Trustees acting herein shall be entitled to one-half of the commission herein provided, to be computed on the amount of the unpaid debt hereby secured at the time of the first advertisement.

In the event the above described property is sold, or title is otherwise transferred except by death, the entire indebtedness hereby secured shall become due and payable, at the option of the holder of said Note. In the event the lender elects to allow this loan to be assumed, it shall not relieve the maker of the Note from any liability.

It is understood and agreed that upon payment of all of the said principal and interest, and the fulfillment and performance of all of the covenants and agreements of the said Note and of this Deed of Trust, then upon the request and at the cost of the Grantor, a proper release and discharge of this Deed of Trust shall be executed.

WITNESS THE FOLLOWING SIGNATURE(S) AND SEAL(S):

_____(SEAL)

_____(SEAL)

STATE OF VIRGINIA
COUNTY OF   , to-wit:

   I, the undersigned, a Notary Public in and for the said jurisdiction, do hereby
certify that   whose name(s) is/are signed to the foregoing and attached
Deed of Trust, dated   ,   has/have acknowledged the same before me
in my jurisdiction aforesaid.

   GIVEN under my hand and seal this   day of   , 20   .

_____

NOTARY PUBLIC

SAMPLE JOINT OWNERSHIP AGREEMENT –

not using the shared equity rules.

THIS AGREEMENT is made and entered into on _____,
20____, by and between

_____
_____ ”Non-
Resident”), and/or their assigns, and

_____
_____ ”Resident”).

RECITALS:

This agreement is entered into on the basis of the following facts, understandings
and intentions of the parties:

A.   Non-Resident and Resident intend to acquire, as tenants in common, that
certain real property (the "Property) located and described as:

_____
_____. As tenants
in common, Non-Resident and Resident will each own an undivided interest in
the Property.

B.   Resident intends, upon acquisition of the Property, to occupy the Property
as a residence.

C.   The parties wish to enter into this Agreement in order to set forth their
respective rights and obligations.

NOW THEREFORE, in consideration of the mutual covenants and agreements
contained herein and other valuable considerations, the parties agree as follows:

1.   Ownership. Upon acquisition of the Property, Non-Resident and Resident
shall own undivided interests in the Property, as tenants in common. The
percentages of ownership for Non-Resident and Resident (the Ownership
Interests) are:

Resident: _____%

Non-Resident _____%

2.   Acquisition of the Property.

(a)   The parties intend to purchase the Property for

_____

Dollars (\$_____), in accordance with the terms of the agreement entered into with seller of the Property, and to obtain a loan (the "Mortgage Loan") in the amount of

_____ Dollars

(\$_____). The balance of the purchase price and the closing costs shall be paid in cash (the "Cash Contributions"). The Cash Contributions shall be paid by the parties hereto into escrow for the purchase of the Property on or before the date of said purchase (the "Closing Date"), as follows:

Non-Resident: \$_____

Resident: \$_____

(b) It is expressly agreed that any deductions for federal and/or state income tax purposes generated by payment of closing costs for acquisition of the Property, including loan fees, shall be claimed by Resident and Non-Resident in accordance with the percentages in which they shall have furnished such funds.

3.   Restrictions. Once the parties have acquired the Property, the prior written consent of both parties shall be required before any of the following actions may be taken with respect to the Property:

(a)   Modification, amendment, alteration or extension of the terms of any existing financing on the Property;

(b)   Obtaining any new financing for the Property, or further encumbering the Property, except for any new financing specifically agreed upon at the time the parties acquire the Property;

(c)   Modification of insurance as called for in this Agreement;

(d)   The lease, sale, exchange, conveyance or other disposition of all or any portion of the Property, except as made pursuant to Paragraphs 17(b) and 20.

4.   Waiver of Right to Partition. Each of the parties acknowledges that it would be prejudicial to the interests of the parties if either party were to seek a partition of the Property by court action. Accordingly, each of the parties hereby waives any and all right which he may otherwise have to seek a partition of the Property by court action, without the prior written consent of the other party. The parties further acknowledge that their relationship as co-owners is not a

partnership and neither party shall have any liability for debts or obligations of the other party.

5.   Permitted Uses. Resident shall use the Property as a residence and for no other purpose unless agreed to by Non-Resident.

6.   Prohibited Uses. Resident shall not do or permit anything to be done in or about the Property which will reduce the insurability of the Property or any of its contents. Resident shall not commit or suffer to be committed any nuisance or waste in or upon the Property and shall not use the Property or permit anything to be done in or about the Property which will in any way conflict with any law, statute, ordinance or governmental rule or regulation now in force or which may hereafter be enacted. Resident shall not use the Property for any commercial or business purpose whatsoever except for a home office.

7.   Maintenance. Resident shall, at his sole cost, maintain the Property and every part thereof in good and sanitary conditions and repair. Resident shall repair any and all damage to or in the Property occurring while the Property is held in co-tenancy hereunder, whether or not such damage is covered by insurance. At the termination of this Agreement, the Property shall be in its present condition, normal wear and tear excepted. Provided that repairs to appliances, heating and air conditioning equipment, plumbing and electrical systems, shall be shared by the parties in accord with their ownership interest, after Resident has paid the first $_____ in any one calendar year. When the repairs are due to Resident's negligence, Resident shall be responsible for the full cost. The cost of new and replacement appliances shall be shared equally.

8.   Insurance.

(a)   At all times while the Property is held in co-tenancy hereunder, there shall be maintained at the sole cost of Resident, comprehensive public liability insurance covering the Property, insuring against the risks of bodily injury, property damage, and personal injury liability with respect to the Property with policy limits of not less than $500,000.00 per occurrence.

(b)   At all times while the Property is held in co-tenancy hereunder, there shall be maintained, fire insurance with extended coverage endorsements upon all buildings and improvements located on the Property to not less than one hundred percent (100%) of the full replacement cost thereof from time to time. The right and authority to adjust and settle any loss with the insurer shall be exercisable only by the parties hereto acting jointly. The insurance proceeds received in the event of a casualty shall be used to pay for the restoration and reconstruction of the building and improvements on the Property to the extent necessary.

(c)   Resident shall be responsible for compliance with the terms of the insurance policies required hereunder and shall deliver copies of the policies to Non-Resident. Unless Non-Resident objects in writing within thirty (30) days of receipt of the policy, it shall be deemed in compliance with the terms of this agreement.

9.   Payments of Ownership and Operating Costs. Resident shall, from the funds jointly contributed by the parties, make timely payments of the Mortgage Loan installments, real property taxes, insurance, fees to homeowner or condominium associations, and other costs of ownership and operation of the Property. Non-Resident shall be obligated to contribute to these expenses the amount of

_____

_____. Any deductions for federal and/or state income tax purposes arising from payment of the interest component of the Mortgage Loan installments, real property taxes, personal property taxes and any other items that may be deductible for such purposes, shall be claimed by the parties in accord with the percentage in which they shall have contributed the funds.

10.   Utilities. Resident shall pay for all water, gas, heat, light, power, telephone service and all other services and utilities supplied to the Property during the time the Property is held in co-tenancy hereunder.

11.   Alterations. Resident shall not make or suffer to be made any alterations, additions or improvements to or of the Property or any part thereof without the consent of Non-Resident, except that any alteration, addition or improvement costing less than $200.00 shall not require Non-Resident's consent and shall be deemed to be made as part of Resident's obligation to maintain the Premises pursuant to Paragraph 7 hereof. Nothing in this Paragraph 12 shall impair Resident's obligation to maintain and repair the Property under Paragraph 7 hereof, irrespective of the cost thereof. Should Non-Residents consent, in writing, to any alteration, addition or improvement costing more than $200.00, the costs will be reimbursed to Resident at the time of sale.

12.   Liens. Resident and Non-Resident shall keep the Property free from any liens arising out of any work performed, materials furnished or obligations incurred by Resident or Non-Resident. This also applies to tax liens.

13.   Entry by Non-Resident. While the Property is held in co-tenancy hereunder, Non-Resident may enter the Property only in the following cases:

(a)   In case of emergency;
(b)   To cure defaults by Resident of his obligations under this Agreement;
(c)   To make semi-annual inspections of the property;
(d)   When Resident has abandoned or surrendered the Property;
(e)   Pursuant to court order; or
(f)   Under the circumstances specified in Paragraph 20.

Except in cases of emergency or when Resident has abandoned or surrendered the Property, or if it is impracticable to do so, Non-Resident shall give Resident reasonable notice of its intent to enter and enter only during normal business hours. Twenty four (24) hours shall be presumed to be reasonable notice in the absence of evidence to the contrary.

14.   Eminent Domain. If all or any part of the Property shall be taken or appropriated by any public or quasi-public authority under the power of eminent domain (a "Taking"), any award resulting from such Taking shall be made available to Resident for purposes of restoration. Any remaining cash proceeds shall be distributed to the parties in accordance with Paragraph 17(d)

15.   Additional Contributions / Default . (Note: This section needs to be completely redone if the occupant is not putting any money into the deal. Probably use an escrowed Release and Deed to be held and delivered if there is a default, notice and no cure.)

To the extent that either Resident or Non-Resident shall furnish funds from time to time for any purpose in excess of his share of such costs due to default of the other party, then after thirty (30) days written notice and an opportunity to cure, the party supplying the funds shall have the option to treat such excess as an "Additional Contribution" to capital and increase the percentage of capital ownership of that party in the same ratio as the additional contribution bears to the original total capital contribution. For example, a $1,000.00 contribution would serve to add ten (10) percentage points to a party's percentage of capital ownership if the original capital contribution totaled $10,000.00. A corresponding reduction of ten (10) percentage points would be experienced by the other party. The new percentage of capital ownership is referred to as the "Adjusted Capital Ownership Percentage".

When the Adjusted Capital Ownership Percentage of any party shall equal 0, that party's interest in the property shall terminate. The non-defaulting party may then cause the property to be sold and in the event the default was by the occupant, the occupant shall become a tenant at sufferance and agrees to vacate the property when requested by the Non-Resident. Each party agrees to execute such documents as may be required to effectuate the intent of this paragraph. Resident will execute and deliver a Deed at closing conveying the property to Non-Resident. Non-Resident is authorized to record this Deed should the Adjusted Capital Ownership of Resident fall to zero. Furthermore, each party agrees to hold the other harmless from any claim action or demand resulting from a default under this agreement, including but not limited to any claim from Mortgage Lender(s). Such hold harmless shall also include all costs and attorney's fees incurred.

16.   Termination Events.

(a)   The parties agree to sell the Property and liquidate the co-ownership upon the occurrence of any of the following (the "Termination Events"):

(i)   Either party's delivery to the other of at least ninety (90) days written notice and the expiration of the time period specified in such notice; provided that such notice shall not be given prior to Notice Date of _____.

(ii)   Either party's breach of any covenant, obligation or provision contained in this Agreement, including obligations required to make payments required hereunder or the filing of a petition in bankruptcy on any lien against the property, and the failure to cure such breach within fifteen (15) days of the breach; provided that accepting an adjustment to the parties' ownership percentage shall be deemed to cure a monetary breach.

(iii)   Termination may be made by mutual agreement of the parties prior to the dates set forth above, subject to adjustment of their respective ownership shares on other mutually agreeable terms to compensate the non-terminating party for the losses associated with early termination.

(b)   Upon the occurrence of a Termination Event, the parties shall cause the Property to be sold as soon as practicable thereafter, and in any event, within one hundred and twenty (120) days of the occurrence of such Event. Until settlement, each party shall remain fully liable for all costs and expenses as set forth in this agreement.

(c)   Each of the parties pledges his interest to the other as security for the obligations set forth herein, including all expenses, costs and attorney's fees expended in enforcing this agreement.

(d)   Upon the sale of the Property, the proceeds of sale after deduction of the then Mortgage Loan balance and closing costs shall be allocated as follows:

(i)   First, to the repayment of Additional Contributions not compensated by an adjustment in ownership including costs in enforcing this Agreement and the cost of the Resident's unfulfilled maintenance and repair obligations, together with interest at 15% per annum until paid; and

(ii)   Second, to reimburse the mortgage amortization to the party or parties making the monthly payment; and

(iii)   Third, to pro-rata repayment of the original Cash Contributions and mortgage amortization; and

(iv)   Fourth, to repayment of Resident's actual home improvement costs (not including Resident's labor) and Non-Resident's payments pursuant to paragraph 9; and

(v)   Fifth, to the parties in accordance with their respective Adjusted Capital Ownership Percentages. Notwithstanding the foregoing, if either party shall default or call for termination before the Notice Date specified above, the terminating party shall guarantee a buy-out value of not less than the original purchase price plus agreed improvements, additional contributions and costs of sale.

17.   Appraisal. Upon notice of termination, the parties shall have thirty (30) days to agree on the fair market value of the property. If the parties are unable to reach agreement, then the fair market value (the "Appraisal Value") of the Property shall be determined by fee appraisals to be made by two independent appraisers, one of which shall be selected by Resident and one Non-Resident. Non-Residents shall have the right to inspect the Property prior to the appraisal; and they shall provide the appraisers with a list of those matters, if any, with respect to which Resident has not satisfied his obligations of repair and maintenance. In such event, the appraisers shall determine the Appraisal Value of the Property as if all such matters had been properly repaired or maintained. The Appraisal Value of the Property shall be deemed to be the average of the two appraisal values determined by the appraisers. The parties agree to cooperate in expediting the foregoing procedure to the end that the Appraisal Value be determined within thirty (30) days.

18.   Resident's Option. Within ten (10) days after agreement on a price or receipt from the appraisers of the Appraisal Value (the "Appraisal Notice"), Resident shall have the right and option (the "Resident's Option") to elect to purchase Non-Resident's interest in the Property for a price equal to the share of the net sale proceeds which Non-Resident would have received, had the Property been sold for a price equal to the Appraisal Value less 10% selling costs.

19.   Sale to Non-Resident. In the event:

(a)   Resident does not elect to exercise the Resident's Option, or;
(b)   Resident does not close the purchase of Non-Resident's interest within ninety (90) days after the Termination Event; then Non-Resident may purchase the Property on the same terms less the cost of Resident's unfulfilled repair and maintenance obligations or the Property shall be sold. Both parties are to cooperate fully to accomplish a sale to a third party and agree to list the property with a real estate broker utilizing the Multiple Listing Service to allow a lockbox to be installed, and to make the property available for showing at all reasonable hours.

20.   Distribution of Cash from Refinancing or Insurance. In the event of a refinancing of the Property, or the receipt of any casualty insurance proceeds or condemnation award with respect to the Property to the extent not used to reconstruct the residence on the Property, any cash arising therefrom shall be applied and distributed to the parties just as if it were net proceeds of sale under Paragraph 17(d).

21.   Notices. Any notice or other communication required or desired to be served, given or delivered hereunder shall be in writing and shall be deemed to have been duly served, given or delivered upon personal delivery or upon deposit (within the continental United States) in the United States mail, registered or certified, with proper postage or other charges prepaid and addressed to the party to be notified as follows:

To Non-Resident:

To Resident: At the street address of the Property

or to other such address or addresses of which either party may notify the other party in writing in the manner prescribed herein.

22.   Successors and Assigns. Resident shall not assign, transfer, sell, mortgage, pledge, hypothecate or encumber this agreement or any interest thereon, including Resident's interest as tenant in common in the Property and shall not permit any person other than Resident's immediate family to occupy or use the Property or any portion thereof without the prior written consent of Non-Resident unless Resident is also occupying the Property as a principal residence. Subject to the foregoing restrictions, this Agreement shall inure to the benefit of

and bind the heirs, executors, administrators, successors and assigns of the respective parties hereto.

23.   Waiver of Claims. Non-Resident shall not be liable to Resident and Resident hereby waives any claims against Non-Resident for any injury or damage to any person or property in or about the Property by or from any cause whatsoever.

24.   Indemnification. Each party shall indemnify the other party for all damages and expenses for which the parties may become liable as a result of any act committed by such party in contravention of the provisions of this Agreement. Resident shall hold Non-Resident harmless from, and defend Non-Resident against, any and all claims of liability for any injury or damage to any person or property in, on, or about the Property when such injury or damage shall be caused in part or in whole by the act, neglect or fault of Resident, Resident's agents, employees or invitees.

25.   Entire Agreement. This Agreement contains the entire agreement of the parties with respect to the matters covered herein, and no other agreement, statement, or promise made by any party which is not contained herein shall be binding or valid. This Agreement may be modified or amended only by a written instrument duly executed by both parties hereto.

26.   Attorney's Fees. In the event any party brings legal action, to enforce any of the provisions of this Agreement, the party which does not prevail in such legal action agrees to pay the costs and reasonable attorney's fees of the prevailing party in such legal action.

27.   Severability. The provisions of this Agreement are intended to be severable. If any term or provision of this Agreement is illegal or invalid for any reason whatsoever, such illegality or invalidity shall not affect the validity of the remainder of this Agreement.

28.   Miscellaneous. This Agreement is governed by the laws of the State of Virginia and any question arising hereunder shall be construed or determined according to such law. Headings at the beginnings of each numbered paragraph of this Agreement are solely for the convenience of the parties and are not a part of this Agreement. The waiver by Non-Resident of the breach by Resident of any term, covenant or condition herein contained shall not be deemed to be a waiver of any subsequent breach of the same or any other term, covenant or condition herein contained. Time is of the essence of this Agreement.

29.   Failure to Acquire Property. Notwithstanding any other provision hereof, this Agreement shall term
nate and all deposits made pursuant to Paragraph 2 hereof shall be returned if the Closing Date does not occur within one hundred and eighty (180) days of the date hereof.

30.   NOT A PARTNERSHIP OR SHARED EQUITY FINANCING AGREEMENT The parties acknowledge that it is not their intent to create a Partnership or a Shared Equity Financing Agreement as that term is defined in the Internal Revenue Code. The Non-Resident agrees that no rent is to be paid or implied by this Agreement and that depreciation and other investment deductions are not available and will not be claimed. The Non-Resident's sole return on the investment will be a portion of the profits, if any, upon sale of the property.

IN WITNESS WHEREOF, this Agreement is entered into on the date above.

NON-RESIDENT   NON- RESIDENT

_____   _____

RESIDENT   RESIDENT:

_____   _____

STATE OF

COUNTY/CITY OF   , to-wit:

I, the undersigned Notary Public in and for the jurisdiction aforesaid, do hereby certify that whose name(s) is/are signed to the foregoing Joint Ownership Agreement dated_____, 20____, has/have acknowledged the same before me in my jurisdiction as aforesaid.

GIVEN under my hand and seal this   day of   , 20____.

_____

Notary Public My Commission Expires:

OFFICE LEASE AGREEMENT

THIS AGREEMENT OF LEASE, made this _____ day of _____ , by and between _____ or Assigns, hereinafter referred to as "Landlord", and _____ hereinafter referred to as "Tenant".

W I T N E S S E T H :

PREMISES 1.01. In consideration of the rent hereinafter reserved and of the covenants hereinafter contained, Landlord does hereby lease to the Tenant, and Tenant hereby leases from Landlord part of the building known as

_____which space is hereinafter referred to as the premises, reserving, however, to Landlord space for all pipes and wires leading to and from the portions of the Building not hereby leased, which will not unreasonably interfere with Tenant's use of the premises.

TERM 2.01. The term of the lease shall commence on the
_____ , and shall terminate at 12:00 Midnight on

_____ .

2.02.   If delivery of possession of the premises shall be delayed beyond the date specified above for the commencement of the term of this lease because of any construction by the Landlord of the demised premises and/or the necessary common areas of the building of which the demised premises are a part is incomplete, or for any reason beyond the control of the Landlord, the Landlord shall not be liable to the Tenant for any damage resulting from such delay and the Tenant's obligation to pay rent shall be suspended and abated until possession of the premises is tendered by Landlord to Tenant. In the event of such a delay, it is understood and agreed that the commencement of the terms of this lease shall also be postponed until delivery of possession and that the termination date of the term shall be correspondingly extended.

RENT 3.01. Tenant hereby covenants and agrees to pay during the term hereof a basic rent of _____ payable without deduction, set-off, or demand in equal monthly installments of _____ in advance, on the first day of each calendar month during the term of this lease.

3.02.   If the lease term begins on other than the first day of a month, rent from such date until the first of the next succeeding month shall be prorated on the basis of the actual number of days in each such month and shall be payable in advance.

3.03.   All payments of rent shall be made by check payable to:

_____ or to such other person and place as may be designated in writing from Landlord to tenant from time-to-time.

3.04.   Notwithstanding any of the other rights of Landlord set forth in the lease, during the term of this lease, should the rent or other charges reserved herein remain unpaid on the fifth day after the date when the same ought to be paid, the Landlord may elect to waive such default and Landlord, at its option, may make a service charge for the purpose of defraying the expenses incidental to handling delinquent payments. Such charge shall be in an amount of five percent (5%) of the delinquent rent and charge for each month, or part thereof, during which said rent and charges remain delinquent.

3.05.   No payment by Tenant or receipt by Landlord of a lesser amount than the monthly installments of rent herein stipulated shall be deemed to be other than on account of costs, expenses, late charges, interest or the earliest stipulated rent and/or additional rent; nor shall any endorsement or statement on any check or letter accompanying any check or payment as rent be deemed an accord and satisfaction and Landlord may accept such check for payment without prejudice to Landlord's right to recover the balance of such rent and/or additional rent or pursue any other remedy provided in this lease and/or under applicable law.

COST OF LIVING ADJUSTMENT 4.01. For purposes of this Paragraph 4.01, the term "lease year" shall be the period commencing on the first full month of the term of this lease and ending twelve months from the first day of said first full month, and each successive twelve month period. Each lease year that this lease remains in effect after the first lease year of the term hereof, Tenant shall pay to Landlord as Basic Rent such sums as determined by application of the following formula:

(a)   To the basic rent payable annually during the previous twelve months shall be added that sum representing the resulting amount, if any, after multiplying such Basic Rent payable during the previous twelve months by a fraction, the numerator of which shall be the Consumer Price Index (CPI), now known as the "U. S. Department of Labor Bureau of Labor Statistics Consumer Price index, United States City Average for Urban Wage Earners and Clerical Workers, All Items (1967 = 100)," for the month which is two months prior to the last month of the previous twelve months, and the denominator of which shall be such CPI for the month which is two months prior to the first month of such previous twelve months, and subtracting from such product the Basic Rent payable during the previous twelve months.

OPERATING REGULATIONS 5.01. The Tenant herein agrees that it shall abide by all of the rules and regulations of the

_____.

OPERATING EXPENSE ESCALATIONS 6.01. For the purposes of this lease, operating expense escalations shall be determined as follows:

a.   Condominium Fee Increase. It is understood between the parties that at the time of execution of this lease, the condominium fee for

_____ and that the lease rate was determined on the basis of Landlord paying this fee. Should the condominium fee assessed increase at any time and from time-to-time over the life of this lease, then and in that event the Tenant will, upon written notice from Landlord with a certified copy of the new assessment attached thereto, commence immediately to pay only the increase over the base quarterly condominium fee presently assessed.
b.   The resulting new basic rent, which in each instance shall in no event be less than the Basic Rent payable during the preceding twelve months shall be payable in twelve equal monthly installments on the first day of each month of the applicable year, beginning with the anniversary month in which the lease commenced.
c.   In the event the CPI is discontinued, the parties hereto shall attempt to agree on an alternative formula and if agreement cannot be reached, the matter shall be submitted to arbitration under the rules of the American Arbitration Association then in effect.

TAXES ESCALATION 7.01. For the purposes of this Article:

a.   The term "taxes" means all taxes, rate and assessments, general and special, public dues, charges and gross receipts, taxes levied and imposed with respect to the land. Building and improvements constructed thereon including all taxes, rates and assessments, general or special, levied or imposed for school, public betterment, general or local improvements. If the system of taxation shall be altered or varied and any new tax or levy shall be levied or imposed with respect to said land, building and improvements, and/or Landlord, in substitution for all or part of said taxes present levied or imposed on immovables in the jurisdiction where the property is located, then any such new tax or levy shall be included within the term "taxes".

b.   The term "base taxes" means the assessed value of said land, building and improvements, multiplied by the then current rate plus other taxes referred to in (a) above, for the tax year during which this lease commences.

c.   The term "tax year" means each successive twelve (12) month period following and corresponding to the period in respect of which base taxes are established, irrespective of the period or periods which may from time to time in the future be established by competent authority for the purposes of levying or imposing taxes.

7.02.   Each year Tenant shall reimburse to Landlord, as additional rent, which shall not be deductible from basic rent or any additional rent or any other rental, Tenant's pro rata share, determined in the manner hereinafter provided, of any increase in taxes for or attributable to the then current tax year over the base taxes (all as defined above).

7.03.   Reasonable expenses incurred by Landlord in obtaining or attempting to obtain a reduction of any taxes shall be added to and included in the amount of any such taxes. Taxes which are being contested by Landlord shall nevertheless be included for purposes of the computation of the liability of Tenant under Paragraph 7.02 hereof, provided, however, that in the event that Tenant shall have paid any amount of increased rent pursuant to this Article 6 and Landlord shall thereafter receive a refund of any portion of any taxes on which such payment shall have been based, Landlord shall pay to Tenant the appropriate portion of such refund. Landlord shall have no obligation to contest, object or litigate the levying or imposition of any taxes and may settle, compromise, consent to, waive or otherwise determine in its discretion, any taxes without consent or approval of Tenant.

7.04.   Nothing contained in this Article shall be construed at any time to reduce the monthly installments of rent payable hereunder below the amount stipulated in Articles 3, 5, or 6 of this lease.

7.05.   It is understood and agreed that Tenant shall not be liable for any increase in the taxes which is occasioned by an increase in the tax assessment due to an expansion of the building by Landlord, nor shall Tenant be liable for any addition to the taxes by reason of Landlord's failure to pay such taxes when due.

7.06.   If the termination date of the lease shall not coincide with the end of a tax year, then in computing the amount payable under this Article 6 for the period between the commencement of the applicable tax year in question and the termination date of this lease, the base taxes shall be deducted from the taxes for the applicable tax year and, if there shall be a difference, such difference prorated on a monthly basis (and pro rata for a portion of a month on the basis of the number of days in that month) shall be payable by Tenant. Tenant's obligation to pay increased taxes under this Article 6 for the final period of the lease shall survive the expiration of the term of this lease.

UPKEEP OF PREMISES 8.01. Tenant accepts the premises in its present "AS IS" condition and agrees to maintain the premises, including plumbing and lights in good order and repair during the term of this lease. Landlord shall be responsible for repairs to the heating, air conditioning and electrical systems, unless damage thereto shall have been caused by the act or neglect of Tenant, in which case the same shall be repaired by and at the expense of Tenant. Tenant shall be responsible for changing the furnace air filter every 60 days.

USE OF PREMISES 9.01. Tenant covenants to use the premises only for the sole and exclusive purpose of offices for carrying on the sole and exclusive business of a _____

TENANT'S AGREEMENT 10.01. Tenant covenants and agrees:

a. To pay to Landlord such basic rent, additional rent and all other rent during the original, and extended terms of this lease thereafter until possession of the premises is redelivered to Landlord in the condition specified.

b. To save Landlord and any managing agent harmless and indemnified from all loss, damage, liability or expense incurred, suffered or claimed by any person in connection with the premises or of said building or of anything therein, or the parking facilities in or adjacent thereto, or of water, steam, electricity, or other agency, or by reason of any injury, loss or damage to any person or property upon the premises and to be answerable for all nuisances caused or suffered on the premises, or caused by Tenant in said building, or parking facilities, or on the approaches thereto.

c. To provide and keep in force during the term of this lease, for the benefit of Landlord and Tenant general liability insurance in any insurance company licensed to do business in the Commonwealth of Virginia in the amount of at least One Hundred Thousand Dollars ($100,000.00) in respect of injuries to any one person; Five Hundred Thousand Dollars ($500,000.00) in respect to any one accident; and Fifty Thousand Dollars ($50,000.00), in respect to property damage in which Landlord shall be named as co-insured; Tenant agrees to deliver certificates of such insurance to Landlord at the beginning of the term of this lease and thereafter not less than five (5) days prior to the expiration of any such policy. In the event that Tenant shall fail promptly to furnish any insurance herein required, Landlord may effect the same and pay the premium therefore for a period of not exceeding one year, and the premium so paid by Landlord shall be payable by Tenant as additional rent on demand.

d. To maintain, at all times during the original and extended terms of this lease at Tenant's sole cost and expense, with Tenant as the party insured, and with waiver by the insurance company of all of its rights to subrogation against Landlord and Landlord's agents and employees, fire and extended coverage insurance (including, but not limited to, theft and mysterious disappearance) in an amount equal at all times to the replacement cost new of all property in the premises owned, leased or paid for in whole or part by Tenant or Tenant's officers, employees or invitees, irrespective of whether or not such property is attached in any manner to the real estate.

e. Not to strip or overload, damage, or deface the premises or hallways, stairways, elevators, parking facilities or other approaches thereto of said building or the fixtures therein or used therewith, nor to permit any holes to be made in any of the same.

f. Not to suffer or permit any trade or occupation or activity to be carried on or use made of the premises which shall be unlawful, noisy, offensive or injurious to any person or property, or such as to increase the danger of fire or affect or made void or voidable any insurance on said building, or which may render any increased or extra premium payable for such insurance, or which shall be contrary to any law or ordinance, rule or regulation from time to time established by public authority.

g. To promptly pay all electric usage charges and cleaning fees associated with the premises, it being understood that this lease does not include cleaning services or utilities except for water and common area cleaning, included in the condominium fee.

h. Not to place upon the interior or exterior of the building or any window or any part thereof or door of the premises any placard, sign, lettering, window covering or drapes except such and in such place and manner, as shall have been first approved in writing by Landlord; not to use any floor adhesive in the installation of any carpeting.

i. To conform to all rules and regulations from time to time established by the appropriate insurance rating organization, and to all rules or regulations from time to time established by Landlord and the Unit Owners Association.

j. To comply at its own expense, with all laws, orders, ordinances, and regulations of Federal, State, County and Municipal authorities and with directions of public officers thereunder, and with Occupational Safety and Health Act, respecting all matters of occupancy, condition or maintenance of the demised premises, whether such orders or directions shall be directed to Tenant or Landlord, and Tenant shall hold Landlord harmless from cost or expense on account thereof.

ALTERATIONS 11.01. Tenant will not paint the premises or permit anyone to make any alterations in or additions thereto, nor will Tenant install any equipment of any kind that will require any alterations or additions to or the use of the water system, heating system, plumbing system, air conditioning system, or the electrical system, nor will tenant install a television or any other antenna on the roof, in the windows or upon the exterior of the premises or air conditioning units of any type, without the prior written consent of Landlord as to each of the foregoing items. If any such alterations or additions are made without such consent, Landlord may correct and/or remove them and restore the premises and Tenant shall be liable for any and all expenses incurred by Landlord in the performance of this work.

TENANT'S WAIVER OF CLAIMS 12.01. Tenant covenants that no claim shall be made against Landlord by Tenant, or by any agent or servant of Tenant, or by others claiming the right to be in the premises or in said building through or under Tenant, for any injury, loss or damage to person occurring upon the premises from any cause other than the negligence of Landlord outside of the demises premises in the common area.

LIEN ON TENANT'S PROPERTY 13.01. Landlord shall have a lien for the payment of the rent aforesaid upon all of the goods, wares, chattels, fixtures, furniture and other personal property of Tenant which may be in or upon the premises, Tenant hereby specifically waiving any and all exemptions allowed by law; and such lien may be enforced on the nonpayment of any installment of rent and/or additional rent by the taking and selling of such property in the same manner as in the case of chattel mortgages in default thereunder; said sale to be made upon ten (10) days' notice served upon the Tenant by posting the same upon the premises or by leaving same at his place of residence; or such lien may be enforced in any other lawful manner at the option of the Landlord.

ASSIGNMENT AND SUBLETTING 14.01. Tenant covenants not to assign this lease nor to sublet the premises or any portion thereof, nor rent desk space therein, without the consent of Landlord first obtained in writing; however, neither such assignment or subletting nor the consent of Landlord thereto shall release, discharge or affect the liability of Tenant, or any Guarantor as provided in this lease, for the full original and any extended terms hereof, except as otherwise expressly provided herein, any attempted assignment or sublease of this lease by Tenant shall be void.

LANDLORD'S RIGHT OF ACCESS 15.01. Tenant will always provide Landlord with a full set of keys for access to the premises. Landlord may at any time and from time to time enter either to view the premises or to show the same to others, or to make repairs to said building, or to introduce, replace, repair, alter or make new or change existing connections from any fixtures, pipes, wires, ducts, conduits, or other construction therein, or remove, without being held responsible therefore, placards, signs, lettering, window or door coverings and the like not expressly consented to by Landlord in writing.

15.02. Landlord may, within ninety (90) days next preceding the expiration of the term, enter the premises to place and maintain notices for letting, free from hindrance or control of Tenant, and to show the premises to prospective tenants thereof at times which will not unreasonably interfere with Tenant's business. If Tenant shall vacate the premises during the last month of the term of this lease, Landlord shall have the unrestricted right to enter the same after Tenant's moving to commence preparation for the succeeding tenant or for any other purpose whatever, without affecting Tenant's obligation to pay rent for the full term.

SURRENDER OF POSSESSION 16.01. Tenant covenants, at the expiration or other termination of this lease, to remove all goods and effects from premises not the property of the Landlord, and to yield up to Landlord the premises and all keys, locks and other fixtures connected therewith in good repair, order and condition in all respects, reasonable wear and use thereof and damage by fire or other casualty, not caused by Tenant's act or neglect, only excepted.

FIRE CLAUSE 17.01. This lease is made on condition that, if the premises or any part thereof, or the hallways, stairways or other approaches thereto, be damaged or destroyed by fire or other casualty from a cause, other than tenant's negligence, so as to render said premises and/or approaches unfit for use and occupancy, a just and proportionate part of the rent, according to the nature and extent of the injury to said premises and/or approaches, shall be suspended or abated until said premises and approaches have been put in as good condition for use and occupancy as at the time immediately prior to such damage or destruction, excluding Tenant's improvements and property. Landlord will proceed at its expense and, as expeditiously as may be practicable to repair the damage, unless, because of the substantial extent of the damage or destruction, Landlord should decide not to repair or restore the premises or the building, in which event and at Landlord's sole option, Landlord may terminate this lease forthwith, by giving Tenant a written notice of its intention within ninety (90) days after the date of the casualty.

CONDEMNATION 18.01. This lease shall be terminated and the rental payable shall be abated to the date of such termination in the event of the condemnation of fee simple title or of the lease term of the premises by any competent authority under right of eminent domain for any public or quasi-public use or purpose. The forcible leasing by any competent authority of any portion of said building other than the premises will have no effect whatever upon this lease. In case of any taking or condemnation, whether or not the term of this lease shall cease and terminate, the entire award shall be the property of Landlord, and Tenant hereby assigns to Landlord all its rights, title and interest in and to any such award.

DEFAULTS AND REMEDIES 19.01. It is hereby mutually covenanted and agreed, that:

a. If Tenant shall fail to keep and perform each and every covenant, condition and agreement herein contained and on the part of Tenant to be kept and formed; and

b. If the Tenant shall abandon or evidence any intention to abandon the premises; or

c. If the estate hereby created shall be taken on execution or other process of law; or

d. If Tenant shall petition to be declared bankrupt or insolvent according to law; or

e. If a receiver or other similar officer shall be appointed to take charge of any part of the property of Tenant, or to wind up the affairs of the Tenant, and it is not discharged within thirty (30) days; or

f. If any assignment shall be made of Tenant's property for the benefit of creditors; or

g. If a petition shall be filed for Tenant's reorganization under Chapter X of the Bankruptcy Act;

Then and in each and every such case, at the sole option of Landlord, Tenant's right of possession shall thereupon cease and terminate, and Landlord shall be entitled to the possession of the premises and to remove persons and property therefrom and to re-enter the same without further demand of rent or demand of possession of said premises, either with or without process of law and without becoming liable to prosecution; therefore, any notice to quit or of intention to re-enter being expressly waived by Tenant, and in the event of such re-entry or retaking by Landlord, Tenant shall nevertheless remain in all events liable and answerable for the full rental. Landlord may elect to declare the entire balance of the lease payments, including all costs and attorney fees, immediately due and payable and Tenant shall also be and remain answerable in damages for the deficiency or loss of rent which Landlord may thereby sustain in respect of the balance of the term. Landlord may let said premises for the benefit of Tenant in liquidation and discharge, in whole or in part, as the case may be, of the liability of Tenant under the terms and provisions of this lease. Damages, at the option of

Landlord, may be accelerated and recovered by it at the time of the retaking or re-entry, or in separate actions, from time to time, as said damages shall have been made more easily ascertainable by relettings of the premises, or such action by Landlord may at the option of Landlord be deferred until the expiration of the term, in which latter event the cause of action shall not be deemed to have accrued until the date of the termination of said term.

19.02. All rents received by Landlord in any such reletting shall be applied first to the payment of such expenses as Landlord may have incurred in recovering possession of the premises and in reletting the same, including, but not limited to, Landlord's attorney's fees; second, to the payment of any costs and expenses incurred by Landlord either for making necessary repairs to the premises or in curing any default on the part of Tenant in any covenant or condition herein made binding upon Tenant; and, last, any remaining rent shall be applied toward the payment of rent due from Tenant under the terms of this lease, with interest at 18% per annum, and Tenant expressly agrees to pay any deficiency then remaining. Landlord, however, at its option, may refrain from terminating Tenant's right of possession, and in such case may enforce against Tenant the provision of this lease for the full term thereof.

19.03. Tenant expressly agrees to reimburse Landlord for any expenses (including attorney fees of 20%), Landlord may incur in enforcing the latter's rights against Tenant under this lease, including, but not being limited to, the collection of rent and the securing of possession of the premises.

19.04. Landlord shall have the additional right and remedy of curing any default of Tenant under this lease, and the cost to Landlord of doing so shall be due and payable by Tenant to Landlord upon demand as additional rent.

SUBORDINATION CLAUSE 20.01. This lease shall be subject and subordinate at all times to the lien of any mortgage or deed of trust encumbrance or encumbrances and to any renewal or extensions of any such mortgage or deed of trust, which may now or at any time hereafter be made a lien upon the building and its land of which the premises are a part, or Landlord's interest therein. Tenant shall execute and deliver such further instrument or instruments subordinating this lease to the lien of any such mortgage or deed of trust encumbrance and encumbrances, and attornment agreement, as shall be desired by any mortgagee or party secured or proposed to be secured; and Tenant hereby appoints Landlord the attorney-in-fact of Tenant, irrevocably, to execute and deliver any such instrument or instruments for Tenant.

TENANT HOLDING OVER 21.01. If Tenant shall not immediately surrender possession of the premises at the termination of this lease, Tenant shall become a tenant from month-to-month, provided rent shall be paid to and accepted by

Landlord, in advance at the rate of rental equal to 125% of the amount (including all rent and all additional rent) payable just prior to the termination of this lease, subject to all escalations and additional rent provided throughout this lease; but unless and until the rent is accepted, Landlord shall continue to be entitled to retake or recover possession of the premises as provided in case of default on the part of Tenant, and Tenant shall be liable to Landlord for any loss or damage it may sustain by reason of Tenant's failure to surrender possession of the premises immediately upon the expiration of the term of this lease. If Tenant shall fail to surrender possession of the premises immediately upon the expiration of the term hereof, Tenant hereby agrees that all the obligations of Tenant and all rights of Landlord applicable during the term of this lease shall be equally applicable during such period of subsequent occupancy, whether or not a month-to-month tenancy shall have been created as aforesaid.

WAIVER AND NOTICE 22.01. No waiver of any breach of any covenant, condition, or agreement herein contained shall operate as a waiver of the covenant, condition, or agreement itself, or of any subsequent breach thereof.

MISCELLANEOUS 23.01. The term "Tenant" shall include legal representatives, successors, and assigns (but the provisions of this Paragraph 22.01 do not supersede the provisions of Paragraph 13.01). All covenants herein made binding upon Tenant shall be construed to be equally applicable to and binding upon his agents, employees and others claiming the right to be in the premises or in said building through or under Tenant.
23.02. If more than one individual, firm, or corporation shall join as Tenant, singular context shall be construed to be plural wherever necessary, and the covenants of Tenant to be the joint and several obligations of each party signing as Tenant, and, when the parties signing as Tenant are partners, shall be the obligations of the firm and of the individual members thereof, all jointly and severally liable.
23.03. Feminine or neuter pronouns shall be substituted for those of the masculine form, and the plural shall be substituted for the singular, wherever the context shall require. It is also agreed that no specific words, phrases, or clauses herein used shall be taken or construed to control, limit or cut down the scope or meaning of any general words, phrases or clauses used in connection therewith.

LANDLORD'S SUCCESSORS 24.01. This lease shall likewise be binding upon and shall inure to the benefit of the parties hereto and their respective heirs, personal representatives, successors and assigns; but this sentence in no respect modified the provisions of Paragraph 13.01 of this lease.

ENTIRE AGREEMENT 25.01. This lease contains the entire agreement of the parties in regard to the premises. There are no oral agreements existing between them. Neither Landlord nor any agent of Landlord has made any representations, warranties or promises with respect to the premises, or the building of which the premises is a part, or the land on which the building is located, or the use of any amenities or facilities, except as herein expressly set forth.

NOTICE AND DEMANDS 25.01. All notices required or permitted shall be deemed to have been given on the date placed in any United States Post Office or United States Post Office Box by certified or registered mail, postage prepaid, addressed to Landlord or Tenant, respectively, at the following addresses or to such other addresses as the parties may designate in writing from time to time. LANDLORD:

_____

TENANT: to the premises or:

26.02. Tenant hereby elects domicile at the premises for the purpose of service of all notices, writs of summons, or other legal documents, or process, in any suit, action, or proceeding which Landlord may undertake under this lease.

QUIET ENJOYMENT 27.03. Landlord covenants and agrees with Tenant that upon Tenant paying the rent and additional rent and observing and performing all the terms, covenants and conditions, on Tenant's part to be observed and performed, Tenant may peaceably and quietly enjoy the premises hereby demised subject, nevertheless, to the terms and conditions of this lease, and to the mortgages and deeds of trust secured upon the land and/or building of which the premises is a part.

GOVERNING LAW 28.01. This lease shall be construed and governed by the laws of the Commonwealth of Virginia. Should any provisions of this lease and/or its conditions be illegal or not enforceable under the laws of said Commonwealth, it or they shall be considered severable, and the lease and its conditions shall remain in force and be binding upon the parties as though the said provisions had never been included.

FORCE MAJEURE 29.01. Each party shall be excused from performing any obligation or undertaking provided for any and all items of rent and additional rent as the same becomes due under the applicable provisions of this lease) for so long as such performance is prevented or delayed, retarded or hindered by act of God, fire, earthquake, flood, explosion, action of the elements, war, invasion, insurrection, riot, mob violence, sabotage, inability to procure or general shortage of labor, equipment, facilities, materials or supplies in the open market, failure of transportation, strike, lockout, action of labor unions, a taking, requisition, laws, orders of government or civil or military or naval authorities, or any other cause, whether similar or dissimilar to the foregoing, not within the reasonable control of the party prevented, retarded, or hindered thereby, including reasonable delays for adjustments of insurance.

FIXTURES 30.01. Tenant shall, upon the expiration or sooner termination of the lease term, surrender to the Landlord, together with the leased premises, any and all replacements, changes and additions thereto, and fixtures and improvements constructed or placed by Tenant thereon, with all equipment in or appurtenant thereto, except trade fixtures removable without any damage to or exposure of nail or screw holes or adhesives in the premises. Any such trade fixtures which Tenant has the right to remove under the foregoing provisions, or personal property belonging to Tenant or to any assignee or subtenant, if not removed at such termination and if the Landlord so elects, shall be deemed abandoned and become the property of the Landlord without any payment or offset therefor. If the Landlord shall not so elect, the Landlord may remove such fixtures or property from the premises and store them at the Tenant's sole risk and expense. The Tenant shall repair and restore, and save the Landlord harmless from any and all damage to the leased premises caused by such removal, whether by the Tenant or by the Landlord.

SECURITY DEPOSIT 31.01. Tenant has delivered to Landlord _____, which amount shall be retained by the Landlord as security for the faithful performance of all of the covenants, conditions and agreements of this lease, but in no event shall the Landlord be obligated to apply the same on rents or other charges in arrears or on damages for the Tenant's failure to perform the said covenants, conditions, and agreement; the Landlord may so apply the security at its option; and the Landlord's right to the possession of the premises for non-payment of rent or for any other reason shall not in any event be affected by reason of the fact that the Landlord holds this security. The said sum, if not applied toward the payment of rent in arrears or toward the payment of damages suffered by the Landlord by reason of the defendant's breach of the covenants, conditions, and agreements of this lease, is to be returned to the Tenant when this lease is terminated, according to these terms, and in no event is the said security to be returned until the Tenant has vacated the premises and delivered possession to the Landlord.

In the event that the Landlord repossesses said premises because of the Tenant's default or because of the Tenant's failure to carry out the covenants, conditions and agreements of this lease, the Landlord may apply the said security on all damages suffered to the date of said repossession and may retain the said security to apply on such damages as may be suffered or which accrue thereafter by reason of the Tenant's default or breach.

EVIDENCE OF CONTINUING VALIDITY 32.01. Tenant shall, without charge, at any time and from time to time hereafter, within ten (10) days, request of Landlord, certify by a written instrument duly executed and acknowledged to any mortgagee or purchaser, or proposed mortgagee or proposed purchaser, or any other person, firm or corporation specified by Landlord, as to the validity and force and effect of this lease, in accordance with its tenor, as then constituted, as to the existence of any default on the part of any party thereunder, as to the existence of any offsets, counterclaims, or defenses thereto on the part of Tenant, and as to any other matters as may be reasonably requested by Landlord.

IN WITNESS WHEREOF, Landlord has hereunto set his hand and affixed his seal and Tenant has hereunto set his hand and affixed his seal, and has caused it's corporate name to be hereunto subscribed and its corporate seal to be hereunto affixed, as the case may be, all on the day and year first above written.

Tenant: Landlord:

_____   _____

DEED OF LEASE

THIS DEED OF LEASE made this _____ day of   ,   , by and between:
TENANT(S):

LANDLORD(S):

W I T N E S S E T H:

1. ADDRESS OF PROPERTY, TERM/RENT. THAT IN CONSIDERATION
of the premises, rents and covenants herein expressed, Landlord hereby leases to
Tenant and Tenant rents from Landlord, upon the terms and conditions herein set
forth, the certain unfurnished property known as   , for
the term commencing on the   day of   and ending on the   day of
for the total sum during the term of   , payable as follows: the first
installment of   covering the period   , through   ,   due
before occupying the premises and acknowledged as received with application.
Subsequent installments of   are due on the first day of each calendar
month thereafter without notice, demand or deduction.

   Tenant here with deposits with Landlord a Security Deposit of   to secure
his full and faithful performance of all covenants and conditions of this Lease.
This sum shall be returned to Tenant, without interest, within forty-five (45) days
after Tenant vacates the property, less any expenses caused by any breach of any
condition of this Lease and any sum due from Tenant, including utility bills, but
not until final water and electric bills are paid. This deposit shall not be used or
applied as a substitute for rent, under any circumstances.

2. PAYMENTS. Rent shall be payable to:

3. OCCUPANT'S USE. Tenant will use said property as a single family
residence for one person and for no other purpose or additional number of persons
whatever, except children born hereafter and temporary guests, without prior
written consent of Landlord. Temporary guests are those persons who occupy
property for no more than two (2) weeks during any twelve (12) month period.
This Lease shall not be assigned nor any portion of the premises sublet without
prior written consent of Landlord.

4. GOOD REPAIR. Except as otherwise provided herein, Landlord will maintain the said property in good repair and tenantable condition and will be responsible for all major repairs not due to the fault or negligence of the Tenant during the continuance of this Lease. Repairs or replacement of equipment provided due to normal wear and tear shall be at the expense of the Landlord.

EQUIPMENT PROVIDED (Landlord to maintain):

EQUIPMENT ON PREMISES IN "AS-IS" CONDITION:

5. PETS. Tenant shall not keep or allow pets on premises without written consent of Landlord.

6. POSSESSION OF PREMISES. In the event that Landlord is unable to deliver possession of the premises at the commencement of the tenancy, the Landlord agrees to use whatever efforts are, in his determination, reasonable to secure possession of the premises for Tenant, including the recovery of possession as against a former occupant wrongfully holding over, but in no event, except for the willful and deliberate misconduct of Landlord, shall Landlord be liable to Tenant for any delay in possession. Tenant shall have no responsibility to pay rent for the time elapsing from the beginning of the term of this Lease until the premises are available for occupancy of Tenant.

7. CONDITION OF PROPERTY. Tenant has made an inspection of the property, and Tenant agrees that the property is in a fit and habitable conditions, except for such damages or malfunctions as have been itemized in writing on a record made by Tenant and Landlord. A copy of such record shall be retained by Tenant and Landlord.

8. DEFAULT OF RENT. In the event that Tenant fails to pay when due any installment of rent, or additional rent, and such rent, or additional rent, is not paid within five (5) days after written notice by Landlord, in addition to other remedies provided by law, Landlord may terminate Tenant's right of possession. Upon such termination, Landlord shall be entitled to possession of the property, to any unpaid rent or additional rent, to recover any damages sustained, including the rent while the property is vacant and any costs of reletting the property, and to such attorney's fees as may be recoverable by law.

If any installment of rent is not paid at the time and place agreed upon, although no formal or legal demand shall have been made for the same or if any of the covenants, conditions or agreements herein contained shall not be performed or observed by the Tenant, according to their full tenor and effort, or in case the leased premises shall be deserted or vacated, then in either or any of said events the Landlord may proceed to recover possession of said premises in accordance with the law governing proceedings between Landlord and Tenant.

9. ATTORNEYS' FEES AND ENFORCEMENT. Tenant further covenants and agrees that in the event of their default in any installment or rent, or in the event of their breach of any covenant or condition hereof, that they will reimburse the Landlord for any money expended by Landlord for reasonable attorneys' fees or other costs which may be incurred to enforce this lease, such reasonable attorneys' fees being twenty percent (20%) of any sums owed to Landlord by Tenant. In addition, as compensation for damages suffered, Landlord may collect a fee of $39.75 (5% of rent due) for any rent check received after the 5th day of the month or for any dishonored check. Should any of Tenant's rent checks be dishonored, Landlord may require all future payments to be by certified or cashiers check or money order.

10. PLUMBING AND APPLIANCES. Tenant shall keep the premises, including all plumbing fixtures, facilities and appliances clean and safe and shall unstop and keep clear all waste pipes, drains and water closets. At the termination of the Lease all appliances and equipment must be in good working order and shall be operative and that the premises will be in good clean condition, ordinary wear and tear excepted. All utility services shall be ordered disconnected and all final bills paid by Tenant before any part of the security deposit can be returned. The Tenant is responsible for loss or damage from freezing or water pipes or plumbing fixtures or from the stopping of water closets and drains which shall be repaired at the expense of the Tenant.

11. USE AND REPAIR OF FACILITIES. Tenant shall use in a reasonable manner all electrical, plumbing, sanitary, heating, ventilating, air conditioning and other fixtures, facilities and appliances in the premises, and Tenant shall be responsible for repairing them at their expense for any damage caused by their failure to comply with this requirement.

12. DAMAGING PROPERTY. Tenant shall not deliberately or negligently destroy, deface, damage, impair or remove any part of the premises (including fixtures, facilities and appliances) or permit any person to do so whether known by the Tenant or not, and Tenant shall be responsible for any damage caused by their failure to comply with this requirement.

13. GENERAL MAINTENANCE. Tenant shall, at their own expenses: (a) keep up and preserve in good condition any lawns, trees, vines, shrubbery and gardens and keep any fences and walks in good repair, natural wear and tear excepted; (b) remove leaves, sticks and other debris that accumulate on the property; (c)

promptly remove ice and snow as necessary and/or required by local ordinance; (d) keep gutters, downspouts and exterior drains cleared and clean of leaves, needles and other debris; (e) furnish their his own light bulbs, furnace filters and fuses; (f) change furnace filters every 60 days; (g) replace all faucet washers as necessary; (h) replace or repair all broken or damaged glass, screens, flooring, wood, plaster, drywall and locks occurring during their tenancy; (i) to keep in a state of good and substantial repair and cleanliness all parts of the property, including equipment and appliances furnished therein, and keep property free from objectionable features, nuisances and hazards.

Any repairs or replacements of property, equipment or appliances necessary due to the negligence by acts of commission or omission of the Tenant, their family, guests or employees, shall be paid by the Tenant. Tenant will not place any heavy articles in property, including water beds, without the written consent of the Landlord.

14. NOTICE OR DEFECTS OR MALFUNCTION. Tenant will give Landlord prompt notice of any known defect, breakage, malfunction or damage to or in the structure, equipment or fixtures in or on said property. This covenant, however, does not obligate, and is not to be understood, interpreted construed or in any way to imply that Landlord is obligated or expected to repair or correct such defect, breakage, malfunction or damage except as provided for in Paragraph 5 ("Good Repair"). Tenant shall be responsible for all secondary or consequential damage caused by their failure to comply with this paragraph.

15. TENANT CONDUCT. Tenant shall conduct themselves and require other persons on the premises with their consent, whether known by the Tenant or not, to conduct themselves in a manner that will not disturb their neighbors' peaceful enjoyment of their premises, and the Tenant further covenants and agrees that they will not use nor permit said premises to be used for any improper, illegal or immoral purposes, nor will they use, permit, or suffer the same to be used by any person or persons in any noisy, dangerous, offensive, illegal or improper manner.

Tenant shall comply with all obligations primarily imposed upon tenants by applicable provisions of building and housing codes materially affecting health and safety. Tenant will not install or use, or permit to be installed or used, any equipment of any kind that will require water, heating electrical, sewerage,, drainage or air conditioning systems of the said property, without prior written consent of the Landlord, and the permission of any governmental agency or public laws. The Tenant will not use or keep in the dwelling any explosives, or inflammable or combustible materials which would increase the rate of fire insurance on the premises. Tenant agrees to abide by all rules and regulations of the

16. SMOKE DETECTORS. It shall be the responsibility of Tenant to check Smoke Detectors periodically during the tenancy and replace batteries as necessary to keep the Smoke Detectors in proper working condition and to report any malfunctions in said Smoke Detectors to Landlord in writing. Landlord assumes no responsibility or liability for any non-reported malfunctions to or misuse of Smoke Detectors by the Tenant which results in injury or damage to the leased premises.

17. REDECORATING AND ALTERATIONS. Tenant shall obtain written permission before redecorating and shall not make any alterations, additions or improvements without first obtaining Landlord's written consent and such alterations, etc., shall, at the option of the Landlord, remain with the property or be removed by Tenant and premises returned to original condition at the expense of Tenant.

18. TRASH REMOVAL. Tenant shall provide appropriate receptacles for the collection, storage and removal of garbage, rubbish and other waste and arrange for the removal of same. Trash removal fees are included in the Homeowner's Association fees, and are therefore, not an obligation of the Tenant.

19. UTILITY CHARGES, DUES AND FEES. Tenant will pay all utility charges, including but not limited to gas, electricity, and telephone. Said utility charges will commence on the effective day of this Lease. Landlord is to pay any and all association dues, homeowner dues, condominium dues, etc., unless otherwise agreed upon.

20. NOTICE OF ABSENCE. Tenant shall give Landlord notice of an anticipated extended absence of Tenant from the property in excess of seven (7) days. During any such absence of Tenant, Landlord may enter the property at times reasonably necessary to protect the property and any possessions of Lessor on or in the property.

21. ACCESS TO PROPERTY BY LANDLORD AND HIS DULY DESIGNATED REPRESENTATIVES. Upon reasonable notice to tenant and at reasonable times, Landlord and/or his duly designated representatives may enter the premises in order to (a) inspect the property, (b) make necessary repairs, decorations, alterations or improvements, (c) supply necessary or agreed services, (d) exhibit the property to prospective or actual purchaser or tenants, mortgagees, appraisers, workmen or contractors, and (e) in addition, sixty days preceding the expiration or termination of said term, Tenant will allow a "for rent" or a "for sale" sign to be placed on the property, along with a lockbox containing a key to the main entrance for prospective tenants' and agents' access.

22. RIGHTS OF LANDLORD UPON BREACH OF LEASE BY TENANT. If Tenant refuses to allow access to Landlord as provided in the preceding

paragraph, Landlord may obtain injunctive relief to compel access or may terminate this Lease or may collect rent for an additional 30 days after the termination of this Lease. In either case, Landlord may recover damages sustained and reasonable attorneys' fees. After termination of this Lease, whether by expiration of the term or by termination by Landlord upon breach by Tenant, the property shall be promptly vacated by Tenant, all items of personal property of Tenant shall be removed, and the property shall be left in good and clean order, reasonable wear and tear excepted. Utilities must be disconnected and all final bills paid and receipts of proof provided.

If Tenant fails to so vacate the property, landlord may bring an action for possession and damages against the Tenant, including reasonable attorneys' fees. In the event Tenant breaches the provisions of Paragraph 21, notwithstanding other remedies of Landlord, Tenant agrees to pay as stipulated and agreed damages, and as partial compensation for Landlord's inability to rent and show the property a sum equal to double the rent which would have been due for the period commencing with the default until the end of the Lease term or the time Tenant vacates the property, whichever last occurs.

If rules and regulations imposed by Landlord, or if any bankruptcy or insolvency proceedings are filed by or against Tenant (or a receiver or trustee is appointed for his property), or if the premises are vacated or abandoned, Landlord shall be entitled to avail himself of all rights and remedies to which he may be entitled, either at law or in equity (including, but not limited to, the right to terminate this Lease and recover possession) and Landlord shall be also entitled to recover reasonable attorneys' fees and costs as allowed by law.

Landlord's waiver of one default by Tenant shall not be considered to be a waiver of any subsequent default. Tenant waives the benefit of any exemption under the homestead, bankruptcy, and any other insolvency law as to their obligations in this Lease.

23. LIENS UPON PROPERTY. The Tenant has no authority to incur any debt or to make any charge against the Landlord or assign or create any lien upon the said leased property for any work, utilities or materials furnished to same.

24. DESTRUCTION AND CASUALTY. If said property shall be partially damaged by fire or other cause without the fault and neglect by Tenant, the damage shall be repaired by and at the expense of Landlord and the rent, according to the extent that the property is rendered untenantable, shall be adjusted or suspended until such repairs are completed. If the said property is damaged by fire or other cause to such extent that Landlord shall decide not to restore the property to the former condition or Landlord shall decide to demolish the structures on said property, then and in either of such events, Landlord shall

have the option to terminate this Lease by written notice to Tenant, and the term of this Lease shall terminate on the day such notice is given with the balance of the rent due hereunder adjusted to the date of such termination. It shall be the responsibility of the Tenant to obtain an insurance policy which provides public liability coverage and also provides for the protection of Tenant's personal property.

25. WAIVER OF BREACH. No waiver or oversight of any breach of any covenants, condition or agreement herein contained, or compromise or settlement relating to such a breach shall operate as a waiver of the covenant, condition or agreement itself, or any subsequent breach thereof.

26. PROPERTY UNFIT FOR HABITATION. If the whole, or any part, of said property should be declared, posted or be the subject of formal notice, by or pursuant to any governmental authority or law, that it is unfit, unsafe, uninhabitable, unsuitable or not lawfully usable for the purpose or persons under this Lease, Landlord shall have the option of eliminating or correcting the cause thereof, if such can be done, and Landlord elects to do so, or terminating this Lease from the date Landlord gives notice to Tenant of such termination or from the date Landlord is compelled by law to terminate further occupancy or use of said property, whichever date is earlier, and the remaining rent due hereunder shall be proportionately adjusted to the effective date of such termination.

27. CONDEMNATION. If the whole or any part of said property shall be taken or condemned pursuant to any governmental authority for any public or quasi-public use or purpose, the term of this Lease shall cease and terminate form the date when the possession of the part so taken or condemned shall be required for such use or purpose, and the remaining rent due hereunder shall be proportionately adjusted to the effective date of such termination.

28. FAILURE TO FULFILL COVENANTS. It is specifically covenanted and agreed between the parties hereto that these presents are executed upon each and all of the conditions, covenants and agreements contained herein, and that if the Tenants, or their executors, administrators, family or invitees do or shall neglect, fail or refuse to perform or observe any of the covenants, conditions, agreements, or undertakings herein contained or if said premises shall be deserted or vacated, then and in any of the said case, in addition to other remedies therefore provided by law, the Landlord may lawfully forthwith or any time thereafter, enter into and upon the said premises, or any part thereof, by force or other wise and without being liable to any prosecution, suit or damages therefore, and repossess the same and expel the Tenant or those claiming under through him and remove their effects without demand or notice, and without prejudice to any remedies which might otherwise be used for arrears of rents, or preceding breach of covenant, and this Lease shall terminate and end, and the Tenant hereby specifically agrees that

they will indemnify the Landlord, its successors or assigns, against all loss or deficiency of rent or other payments which they may incur by reason of such termination, and without further notice or consent of the Tenant may proceed to relet said premises.

The Tenant also agrees that all property on the said premises and for thirty (30) days after removal, shall be liable to distress for rent, and waives the benefit of all laws exempting any of their property from levy and sale, either on distress for said rent or on judgment obtained in a suit therefore.

29. TENANT NEGLECT AND COSTS. If at any time during the term of this Lease, or any renewal or extension thereof, Landlord should be required by any governmental authority to make repairs, alterations or additions to said property or its equipment, caused by the use or neglect thereof by Tenant, tenant hereby agrees to have said repairs, alterations or additions made at Tenant's risk, cost and expense, and if Tenant fails to do so promptly, Landlord shall have the option of terminating Tenant's possession or causing such repairs, alterations or additions to be made, and the cost of same, plus ten percent (10%) thereof, shall be considered as additional rent for said property and payable forthwith by Tenant. The provisions of this paragraph shall be in addition to and shall not prevent the enforcement of any claim Landlord may have against Tenant for any other breach or damages under this Lease.

30. UNENFORCEABLE CLAUSES. All individual provisions, paragraphs, sentences, clauses, sections and words in this Lease shall be severable and if any one or more such provision, section, paragraph, sentence, clause or word is determined by any court, administrative body, or tribunal having proper jurisdiction to be in any way unenforceable, or to be in any way violative of or in conflict with any law of any applicable jurisdiction, such determination shall have no effect whatsoever on any of the remaining paragraphs, provisions, clauses, sections, sentences, or wording of this Lease.

31. LIABILITY FOR PERSONAL OR PROPERTY DAMAGE. All persons and personal property in or on said property shall be at the sole risk and responsibility of Tenant. Landlord shall not be liable for any damage or injury to said persons or personal property arising from the negligence, acts or omission of acts of any persons or entity, or from roof, wall floor, door or window water leaks, or from the freezing, bursting, leaking, or heating or plumbing fixtures, or from electric wires or fixtures, or form any other cause whatever, latent or patent. In summary, the Landlord shall not be liable for any injury or damage whatever in or on said property; and Tenant hereby expressly and without reservation covenants and agrees to save Landlord harmless in all such matters, unless such injury or damage is committed deliberately and with malice by Landlord.

32. It is the responsibility of Tenant when property is vacated, to thoroughly clean, including stove, refrigerator, kitchen cabinets, sink, and counter top, and to remove and have hauled away all trash. Carpeting to be professionally cleaned and receipt given to landlord. Walls and woodwork must be left free from marks, blemishes, holes and other defacements, and be reasonably clean.

THIS AGREEMENT is the entire agreement between the parties, and no modification or addition to it shall be binding unless signed by the parties hereto. The covenants, conditions and agreements contained herein are binding upon and shall inure to the benefit of the parties hereto and their respective heirs, executors, administrators, personal representatives, successors and assigns. Tenants signing this Agreement shall be jointly and severable liable. Whenever the context so requires, the singular member shall include the plural, the plural the singular, and the use of any gender shall include all other genders.

WITNESS the following signatures and seals:

TENANT(S):   LANDLORD(S)

LETTER OF INTENT TO BUY AND SELL REAL ESTATE

This letter of intent is between   (Buyers) and   (Sellers) for the Property known as:

to include those fixtures, appliances and items determined in the final agreement.

It is the intent of the parties to negotiate in good faith a contract for the purchase and sale of the Property. If they do not reach agreement on a contract by   , either party may declare negotiations ended and this letter of intent shall be of no further force and effect. The general terms of the agreement are as follows:

Price:

Contingent on Buyer obtaining a loan of:

Seller's contribution toward Buyer's closing costs:

Deposit:

Closing date: Possession date:

Optional item: Seller will grant Buyer or Buyer's home inspector access to the property during negotiations and the final contract is contingent on the results of Buyer's home inspection and such other inquiries as Buyer may make.

Optional item: Seller to provide financing to Buyer subject to Seller's acceptance of Buyer's credit and financial information.

Signature lines for Buyer and Seller

ASSIGNMENT OF CONTRACT

The Assignment of Contract is made this _____ day of
_____, 20____, by and between:

Assignor: _____ , and

Assignee: _____ , and

Seller: _____

W I T N E S S E T H :

WHEREAS, Assignor is the Buyer under a certain Contact dated
_____ between Assignor and (Seller) for the purchase and sale
of: _____(Property)
all as more particularly set forth in the Contract attached hereto as Exhibit A and
incorporated by reference, and

WHEREAS, Assignee desires to purchase all of Assignor's right title and interest
in the said Contract, and

WHEREAS, Seller has consented to the assignment and agrees to release the
Assignor of further liability under the contract

NOW THEREFORE, in consideration of the mutual covenants and conditions
contained herein the parties do agree as follows:

1. Assignor does hereby sell and assign all of its right title and interest in the said
Contract to Assignee.

2. In consideration of the transfer, Assignee agrees to pay Assignor the sum of

_____ payable

_____ with this
Assignment and the balance at settlement.   Assignee further agrees to do all
things required of Assignor under said Option and to hold Assignor harmless from
any default of Assignee.

3. Assignor and Assignee agree to execute such other documentation as may be
necessary to fully and finally transfer all interest in the Contract and Property to
Assignee.

4. Assignor warrants as follows:

a) There are no defaults or defenses to full performance under the Contract.

b) There are no undisclosed oral or written modifications to the Contract.

c) All bills for improvements and other work have been or will be paid and there will be no claims made against Assignee or the Property for work performed.

5. Seller joins in this assignment to evidence consent and to release Assignor from any further liability in connection with the Contract.

This Agreement contains the full and final understanding of the parties and may not be modified except in writing.

Entered into this _____ day of _____, 1997

Assignors: Assignees:

_____   _____

_____   _____

Sellers:

_____

_____

SECTION FIVE - TEN SECRETS

TEN SECRETS YOUR BUILDER DOESN'T WANT YOU TO KNOW

SECRET #1 I HOLD ALL THE CARDS

Builder contracts are notoriously one-sided. Builder's attorneys have done a great job of plugging loopholes and eliminating every protection the normal buyer would expect.

Always have an independent attorney review the builder's contract with you, before you sign. You may not be able to negotiate many changes but at least you'll understand what you are up against.

SECRET #2 WHAT YOU SEE IS NOT WHAT YOU GET

Model homes do not represent the final product accurately. Decorating and finishing make a world of difference. Don't fall in love with the decorating.

Model homes often contain every upgrade the builder offers. Be sure you understand what is standard and what is an upgrade.

If the house hasn't been started yet, watch out for clauses that allow the builder to move the house, reverse the floor plan or rearrange the lot.

SECRET #3 I CAN SPEND YOUR DEPOSIT

Many states have no restriction on the builder's use of your deposit. Builders treat it as an advance payment and can spend it on another property.   If the builder spends it and later goes out of business, your money is lost. Insist on having your attorney or real estate agent hold the deposit, if you can.

SECRET #4 I HAVE NO IDEA WHEN YOUR HOUSE WILL BE READY

Beware of delivery date promises. The earlier you buy in the construction schedule, the less accurate the forecast. Many builder contracts give up to two years leeway on the delivery date. If the delivery date is important to you, add a clause to the contract giving you the right to cancel or collect damages for late delivery.

SECRET #5 I CAN CHANGE THE LANDSCAPING AND SUBSTITUTE MATERIALS

Most builder contracts give the builder latitude to change landscaping or grading. Some even allow the builder to make changes on your property after settlement.

Most builders also retain the right to substitute materials, kitchen cabinets, bathroom fixtures and appliances without notice to you.

You should ask for notice of any changes and limit the builder's right to make changes without consulting you on the substitute.

SECRET #6 I AM IN CAHOOTS WITH THE LENDER AND SETTLEMENT AGENT

Many builders have arrangements with lenders and settlement agents. Some are innocent and some are not. Some are unavoidable.

If the builder's settlement agent will conduct the closing, you have no one in your corner to protect you. Be sure to have your own attorney review settlement documents on your behalf.

Do not assume the builder's lender will give you the best rate and terms. Often the builder is getting a referral fee from the lender and that fee may actually increase the cost of your loan.

SECRET #7 YOU WON'T BE ABLE TO SELL YOUR HOUSE UNTIL I AM SOLD OUT OF NEW HOMES

Many buyers prefer a new home and will pass by yours. Builders are much better at marketing and often offer attractive financing or other incentives. Think twice if there is any chance you might have to move before the builder is finished selling his homes. On the other hand, the first buyers in a subdivision generally buy at lower prices than those who come later.

SECRET #8 IF I DON'T PAY A CONTRACTOR, HE MAY FILE A LIEN AGAINST YOUR PROPERTY

Many states recognize what are called "mechanic's liens." These laws protect unpaid workers, sub-contractors and suppliers by allowing them to file a lien against property. Protect yourself by insisting the builder provide you with lien waivers and affirmative mechanic's lien coverage in your title insurance policy.

SECRET #9 I MAKE BIG MONEY ON UPGRADES

Builder upgrades such as decks, garage door openers and landscaping carry heavy markups. There is an advantage in having the builder do the work and financing the cost in your mortgage. However, you will almost always get a much better price from an independent contractor.

SECRET #10 IF YOU DON'T GET YOUR LOAN, YOU MAY BE IN DEFAULT

Many builder contracts have no financing contingency. The loan is totally your responsibility. Be careful even if you are sure you qualify today. If the delivery is late and interest rates have risen so you no longer qualify, you could be in default even though the delay was caused by the builder.

TEN SECRETS YOUR LENDER DOESN'T WANT YOU TO KNOW

SECRET #1 I HAVE NO IDEA WHERE THE MONEY WILL COME FROM

You think of a loan as a liability. The person who holds your loan thinks of it as an income stream. To that lender or investor, your loan is an asset. An asset may be bought and sold. Most lenders sell their loans. There are a few lenders who hold their own loans and they are called "portfolio lenders." Your local bank is probably a portfolio lender. A mortgage company will almost always sell its loans.

If your loan is sold, it doesn't mean the lender does not like you. If your loan has already closed, your terms remain the same and you merely make your payments to a different address. However, sometimes loans get sold before they close. This means your friendly loan officer (the salesman who took your application) may drop out of the picture shortly before settlement. Then, you have a new loan underwriter (the person who approves the loan) looking at your application. There may be delays and additional requirements or fees.

How do you protect yourself? Deal only with well-known and well-funded lenders. A mortgage company owned by a bank is probably safe because it will sell the loan to the parent bank. In that case, you would be dealing with the same underwriter and fees. Avoid the mortgage company who takes your application and then "shops" for the money.

SECRET #2 ESTIMATES ARE JUST A GUESS

Your lender should provide you with a good-faith estimate of closing costs. It is a "guesstimate." An experienced loan officer, dealing with a known loan product, should be able to provide a very close estimate of loan fees. If you change loans, or your loan is sold before closing, the fees can change.

There will always be some fees the lender didn't estimate. Lenders usually do not include the cost of optional owner's title insurance. The lender would not include messenger fees or tax prorations. The lender would be guessing at fees charged by the title company or attorney handling the settlement.

Most real estate agents also provide a good faith estimate. Take both estimates and combine the highest figures on each to get a closer approximation of what you will need to close. If you are really concerned, give the estimates to the title company or attorney handling settlement and ask for their estimate.

SECRET #3 THE APR ON YOUR TRUTH IN LENDING FORM IS MEANINGLESS

Remember the days of "add-on" interest and the Rule of 78's? If you don't, it is probably because of the truth in lending form. There was a time when banks had so many convoluted ways of calculating interest it was impossible to tell what a loan really cost. Even today, it is hard to compare the many loan programs available. How can you tell if a loan at 6% with 2 discount points with an increase to 7% after one year and 8% after two years is cheaper than a loan at 7 ½% with one discount point?

In response to all that confusion, the Federal Reserve mandated a Truth in Lending Form and developed a formula to arrive at the Annual Percentage Rate (APR). The formula takes into account rate changes and all fees or discount points are collected in advance. Looking at two loans, the one with the lowest APR is the cheapest. Sound simple? It isn't.

The APR is meaningless because:

1) With an adjustable rate loan, the APR will change depending upon the lender's guess as to what will happen with interest rates over the life of the loan. In the case of an adjustable rate loan, the APR is truly worthless. The rates will be whatever they are and the lender's guess won't help you a bit.

2) Even with a fixed rate loan, cheapest isn't always best for you. In the example above, maybe you don't qualify for a loan at 7 ½% but you do qualify at 6% and you know you'll be getting a promotion so you don't care that the rate will rise to 8% in two years. Even though the 7 ½% loan has the lower APR, it doesn't meet your needs.

3) The APR assumes you will keep the loan for its entire life. Most folks don't. That means, upfront fees the APR spreads over thirty years are paid in a much shorter time. That will raise the true cost of the loan.   As an example, a 7 % loan with two points upfront costs 9% if paid in one year. If those two points are spread over thirty years, the APR will appear much lower. If you know you will move in a few years, look for a loan with fewer upfront fees.

SECRET #4 NO CLOSING-COST LOANS OR "BUNDLED COSTS" COST YOU MORE

If you remember that your loan is someone else's income stream, you will realize that the higher the income stream the more the loan is worth. The higher the interest rate on your loan, the more someone will pay to own it. If your rate is above market, your loan may actually be worth more than the face value. For example, consider a loan returning $10,000 per year. If the prevailing rate of interest is 10%, that income stream is worth $100,000. A $100,000 loan at 10% would be said to trade at "par" the same as its face amount. However, a $100,000 loan at 11% pays an additional $1,000 per year in income and, if the prevailing rate is 10%, that loan will be worth an $110,000.

Therefore, if you to pay a higher interest rate, the lender can sell the loan for more than you borrowed and recoup any closing costs paid on your behalf. The bad news is you are stuck with a loan at a higher rate. Over the life of the loan, those additional charges could be substantial. You saved a few dollars at closing but got stuck with $30,000 of additional payments. Ouch!

"Bundled costs" are just another way of obscuring the facts even more. You don't know what you are paying for individual closing costs and it is all wrapped into a higher payment. This is double- trouble. Ignorance may be bliss – but it carries at a high price.

SECRET #5 YOU CAN'T GET RID OF MORTGAGE INSURANCE

Mortgage insurance is insurance to protect the lender against your default. It does not pay the loan off if you die or become disabled, unless you default. If the mortgage insurance company pays off your loan, they have the right to collect from you whatever they paid out. It is not true insurance but rather an indemnity for the lender required as a condition of the loan when you do not make a large enough down payment.

FHA loans have their own form of mortgage insurance which last about 10 years. Conventional loans with less that 20% down almost always require insurance. So, can you delete the mortgage insurance when your equity reaches 20%? The answer is a very qualified "maybe." Some programs require you to keep the insurance a minimum number of years. The theory is that most of the risk is in the first few years. The mortgage insurance company is entitled to collect premiums over a minimum number of years to compensate for taking a big risk for those first few. Property appreciation may not be enough to get the insurance cancelled because the program says you must have the insurance until you r balance reaches 80% of the original purchase price – not 80% of present value.

Most programs require you to pay for another appraisal to prove your equity has increased. Most don't drop the insurance automatically until 10 years or more.

Ask your loan officer when you apply for your loan. The best time to get rid of mortgage insurance is when you take out the loan in the first place. Many lenders have programs that use a combination of two loans: a first trust at 80% loan-to-value ratio and a second trust of 10%. You put down the same 10% cash but since the first trust is only 80%, it doesn't require mortgage insurance. Expect to pay a higher interest rate on the second loan but the total cost will still be less than mortgage insurance. Also, you could pay off the second loan and end up with a lower mortgage payment. If the second is a home equity line of credit (HELOC) you can pay it back and re-borrow the money with no additional closing costs. HELOC's are a very flexible and attractive way to avoid mortgage insurance and provide for your future needs.

SECRET #6 I AM IN CAHOOTS WITH THE REAL ESTATE AGENT AND TITLE COMPANY

Many lenders have incestuous relationships with real estate companies and settlement agents, also called title companies. That means there are referral fees or other considerations for sending business. That kickback influences their recommendation. You're steered to the place that will profit the lender rather than the one that will do the best job for you.

Sometimes there is no kickback, just companies that have a common ownership. What is wrong with that picture? You have no one in your corner representing you. If the lender, real estate company and title company all have a stake in the outcome, their collective self-interests will be more important than any consideration or concern you may have. For example, I have seen cases where title problems get swept under the rug just so the case can close. Then, you have trouble when you try to sell and find out your title insurance policy won't cover the problem.

SECRET #7 YOUR PRE-QUALIFICATION LETTER IS JUST A PIECE OF PAPER

We call the pre-qualification letter the "Swiss cheese" letter because it is so full of holes. It is not a commitment to make a loan. Read it carefully. It probably contains weasel words like "based on a preliminary review of the information provided to us by the applicant, we believe the applicant will qualify. Subject to verification of income, credit report and appraisal." This is like the unsolicited credit card application you receive saying you are pre-approved for a $50,000 line of credit. If I am pre-approved, why are you asking me to fill out an application?

You should meet with a lender to determine what loan is right for you. Many real estate agents will ask you to pre-qualify. That will help you determine a price range. You may find you can afford more (or less) house than you thought. Just don't mistake that pre-qualification for a commitment.

SECRET #8 HOW NOT TO SHORTEN YOUR LOAN

Heard of the bi-weekly mortgage? They promise to dramatically lower your loan costs because you pay every two weeks instead of once a month. Your loan does indeed pay down quicker and you can knock several years off a thirty year loan. You think since there are two weeks in a month, you are paying the same amount. Magic? No. There are 52 weeks in a year and you pay half a mortgage payment every two weeks. Those 26 half-payments mean you actually make the equivalent of 13 monthly payments a year instead of twelve.

Don't confuse a true bi-weekly with the after-market variety. A true bi-weekly is established with your lender at the beginning. You get the benefit of immediate credit of funds toward your loan and you have the security of knowing who you are paying.

The aftermarket bi-weekly gives you the benefit of making 13 payments but has some serious shortcomings. First, you must rely on the after-market company. Are they bonded, licensed or insured? Some are little more than a kid with a computer. How do you know they will do what they are supposed to? Second, since your loan is only set up to receive monthly payments your bi-weekly payments go into a holding account before being applied. That holding account may or may not pay interest and it certainly won't pay at as high a rate as your loan costs. The after-market bi-weekly company will also charge you a fee to set up and maintain the account.

The major reason a bi-weekly pays your loan off faster is the effect of that thirteenth payment every year. You can get almost the same benefit by making thirteen payments yourself. Take your monthly principal and interest figure and divide it by twelve. Add that amount to your payment each month.

No matter how you choose to pay your loan early, be sure the lender knows what you are doing. I have seen cases where the lender put the extra money in the tax escrow account where it did no one any good. Some payment coupons have a line for "additional principal." Don't trust that alone. Check to be sure the money is going where you want it.

SECRET #9 THE RIGHT WAY TO PREPAY YOUR LOAN

Prepaying a loan does not lower the later payments of a fixed rate loan or entitle you to skip future payments. It just means the loan will pay off sooner. With an adjustable rate loan the term remains the same but the payments go down because the loan is re-calculated every time the rate changes.

Here's a trick I learned a few years ago - it is so ingenious I don't know why everyone doesn't take advantage.

The trick is to set this up when you apply for your loan. Suppose you were going to buy a $100,000 home and put $30,000 down getting a loan for $70,000. Don't do it. Put $20,000 down and get a loan for $80,000. Then, after closing, pay down your loan with the extra $10,000. What happened here?

Borrowing the additional $10,000 would cost you only $66 a month at 7% interest. Prepaying the loan by $10,000 knocks off 102 payments. That is almost 9 years and at 7% saves you over $54,000 in payments. The additional $66 a month for the remaining 258 months only costs you $17,028. Bingo, I just saved you $37,000.

Notice, I made sure you put at least 20% down. That way, you avoid the additional cost of mortgage insurance that could wipe out the savings. This method may work even with mortgage insurance but you'll have to run the numbers yourself.

SECRET #10 DON'T BORROW MONEY FOR LONGER THAN YOU NEED IT

You pay for the use of money. Lenders call the charge interest. And, the longer you want to borrow money the higher the rate of interest you pay. It follows that 30 year loans will carry a rate higher than 5 year loans. If you know you will move in 5 years, you should not pay a premium to borrow for 30. However, taking an ARM is not without risk as the rates can rise dramatically. Don't get caught by borrowing shorter than you really need.

Adjustable rate loans come in many forms. The jargon is that the first number is the fixed period and the second number is the adjustable period. A "7/23" would be fixed for 7 years and then adjust for the remaining 23. Other adjustables include 1, 3 and 5 year ARMs. These adjust every period as stated.

The rate is determined by the "margin" over an "index." The index is the base and the margin is added to the index to get the rate you actually pay. For an index, many are tied to the Treasury rates and you pay a margin of 2 to 2.75 points over whatever the government pays to borrow money. There are also ARMs tied to the London Interbank Offered Rate (LIBOR) an international index and loans tied to the Eleventh Federal Reserve District Cost of Funds (COFI). COFI loans fluctuate with the rates West Coast banks pay their depositors. COFI loans are fairly stable and rates move up slowly and drop quickly because banks are stingy with their depositors. When rates go up, they are slow to raise the rates they pay on savings and checking accounts and vice versa.

ARMs usually feature a low beginning rate but can climb as much as 6 points over the life of the loan. That limit is called the "cap." There is an annual or semi-annual cap and a lifetime cap. A typical annual cap might be 1-2% per year meaning the rate cannot increase or decrease by more than one or two percentage poinst each year. The lifetime cap is an absolute maximum and minimum. Therefore, a one year adjustable with a 2 point cap might start at 6% but could jump to 8% the second year and 10% the third. That assumes interest rates take a dramatic leap upward and is probably not likely. More likely, would be a gradual drift of 6-7-8 for an average of 7 over the three years.

The lifetime cap is usually 5-6%. A loan that starts at 6% might have a lifetime cap of 11-12%. That is a scary jump as it will double the payment. If you think rates will be going up, lock in your low rate.

There is usually a cap on the minimum too. Lenders don't want the rate to go too low!

Watch out for the fact that adjustables often feature a low "teaser rate" which will almost always end up above the regular fixed rate over time. They are truly for the short timer.

SECTION SIX - REAL ESTATE DICTIONARY

Defined words are in all caps.

ABSTRACT - A title abstract is the notes made by a title examiner based on his examination of the land records. These notes are a concise summary of the transactions affecting the property. The title agency produces a BINDER from the information in the abstract.

ACCELERATION CLAUSE - A provision giving the lender the power to declare all sums immediately due and payable upon the happening of an event, such as the sale of the property, or a delinquency in repayment.

ACCRETION - The buildup of land from natural forces such as wind or water.

ACKNOWLEDGMENT - As a verb, the confirmation by a party executing a legal document that this is his signature and voluntary act. This confirmation is made to an authorized officer of the Court or notary public who signs a statement also called an acknowledgment.

ACRE - 43,560 square feet of land.

ADJUSTABLE RATE MORTGAGE (ARM) - A mortgage loan with interest subject to change during the term of the loan.

ADMINISTRATOR - A person appointed by the Court to settle the estate of a person who dies without a will. The feminine form is Administratrix. Compare, EXECUTOR.

ADVERSE POSSESSION - A claim made against land titled in another person based on open, notorious and hostile possession and use of the land to the exclusion of the titled owner.

AMORTIZATION - The periodic principal paydown of a loan.

AMORTIZED LOAN - A loan to be repaid, interest and principal, by a series of regular payments that are equal or nearly equal, without any special balloon payment prior to maturity.

ANNUAL PERCENTAGE RATE - The relative cost of credit including all points or upfront fees along with the regular monthly payments.

APPRAISAL - An estimate of the value of property.

APPROVED ATTORNEY - An attorney authorized by a title insurance company to handle closings and render opinions on their behalf.

APPURTENANCE - Anything attached to the land or used with it that will pass to the new owner on conveyance of the land.

ASSIGNEE - One who receives an assignment or transfer of rights. An assignment of a contract transfers the right to buy property.

ASSIGNOR - The one who assigns to another person.

ASSUMPTION - Taking over a loan and becoming personally liable for the repayment. Compare, SUBJECT TO.

ATTACHMENT - Seizure of property through Court process to repay a debt.

ATTORNEY IN FACT - A type of agency relationship where one person holds a POWER OF ATTORNEY allowing him to execute legal documents on behalf of another. Decisions made by the attorney in fact are binding on the principal.

AUGMENTED ESTATE - To prevent a party from purposely disinheriting a spouse, the surviving spouse can claim a portion of the decedent's augmented estate. The augmented estate includes property given away during life and property sold under terms that were not bone fide and supported by consideration.

BALLOON PAYMENT - An installment payment on a note - usually the final one - which is significantly larger than the other installment payments.

BANKRUPTCY - A provision of Federal Law whereby a debtor surrenders his assets to the Bankruptcy Court and is relieved of the future obligation to repay his unsecured debts. A Trustee in Bankruptcy administers the assets, selling them to pay as much of the debt as possible. If your seller is in bankruptcy, the Trustee in Bankruptcy owns the property and is the party to sign the contract and make decisions.

After bankruptcy, the debtor is discharged and his unsecured creditors may not pursue further collection efforts against him. Secured creditors, those holding deeds of trust or judgment liens, continue to be secured by the property but they may not take other action to collect from the debtor.

BENEFICIARY - A person named to receive a benefit from a TRUST. A contingent beneficiary has conditions attached to this rights, usually that someone else must die first.

BINDER   A title insurance binder is the written commitment of a title insurance company to insure title to the property subject to the conditions and exclusions shown on the binder. The binder is delivered to the lender and the settlement attorney.

BLANKET MORTGAGE - A single mortgage covering more than one piece of property.

BOND - An amount of money, often posted with the Court, to guarantee against loss as a result of a possible claim. For example, if there is a MECHANIC'S LIEN against the property, the owner may post a bond and the lien is removed from the property and the parties argue over the money rather than the property.

BUILDING RESTRICTION LINE - A required set-back within which no building may take place.   This restriction may appear in the original plat of subdivision, restrictive covenants or by building codes and zoning ordinances.

CAVEAT EMPTOR - Buyer beware. The buyer must inspect the property and satisfy himself it is adequate for his needs. The seller is under no obligation to disclose defects but may not actively conceal a known defect or lie if asked.

CERTIFICATE OF SATISFACTION - A document signed by the Noteholder and recorded in the land records evidencing release of a DEED OF TRUST or other lien on the property.

CERTIFICATE OF TITLE - A written opinion by an attorney setting forth the status of title to the property. Certificates of title are no longer in common use.

CHAIN OF TITLE - The series of transactions from Grantor to Grantee as evidenced in the land records.

COINSURANCE - When more than one insurance company shares the risk of a particular transaction or series of transactions. Lenders may require co-insurance on large commercial projects.

COLLATERAL - Property pledged to secure a loan.

CONDEMNATION - Taking of private property for a public use through exercise of the power of EMINENT DOMAIN. The Constitution protects against taking without fair compensation.

CONDOMINIUM - A system of individual FEE SIMPLE ownership of portions (units) in a multi-unit structure, combined with joint ownership of common areas. Each individual may sell or encumber his own unit. Compare, COOPERATIVE.

CONSERVATOR - Also called a Commitee or Guardian, a person designated by the Court to protect and preserve the property of someone who is not able to manage their own affairs. Examples include the mentally incompetent, minors and incarcerated persons.

CONTRACT FOR DEED - A method of financing where title remains in the Seller's name until the Buyer has paid the full purchase price.   A Contract for Deed will normally trigger the DUE ON SALE CLAUSE in a DEED OF TRUST but Veterans Administration regulations specifically allow Contracts for Deed without invoking the DUE ON SALE CLAUSE.

CONVENTIONAL MORTGAGE - A mortgage securing a loan made by investors without governmental underwriting, i.e., which is not FHA or VA guaranteed.

COOPERATIVE - A system of individual ownership of stock in a corporation that in turn, owns the structure. Each owner has an exclusive right to use his individual unit and must pay his portion of the debt encumbering the entire building. Compare, CONDOMINIUM.

COTENANCY - Ownership in the same land by more than one person. See, TENANCY IN COMMON, JOINT TENANTS, TENANCY BY THE ENTIRETIES.

COVENANT - A written agreement or restriction on the use of land or promising certain acts. Homeowner Associations often enforce restrictive covenants governing architectural controls and maintenance responsibilities. However, land could be subject to restrictive covenants even if there is no homeowner's association.

DEED - The written document conveying real property. The Deed must be executed (signed), ACKNOWLEDGED, and DELIVERED to the Grantee. Once recorded at the Courthouse, the original piece of paper is not needed to convey title in the future.

DEED OF TRUST - A voluntary lien to secure a debt deeding the property to Trustees who foreclose, sell the property at public auction, in the event of default on the Note the Deed of Trust secures. Compare, MORTGAGE.

DEFICIENCY JUDGMENT - If the foreclosure sale does not bring sufficient proceeds to pay the costs of sale and pay the note in full, the holder of the note may obtain a judgment against the maker for the difference.

DELIVERY - Final, irrevocable, unconditional and absolute transfer. The Grantor must deliver a DEED to the Grantee. A Deed, signed but held by the Grantor, does not pass title.

DOWER - A spouse's interest in the property of a deceased spouse. Abolished in Virginia and replaced by the AUGMENTED ESTATE concept.

DUE ON SALE CLAUSE - A clause in the DEED OF TRUST that makes the loan non-assumable by providing the noteholder may call the loan immediately due and payable upon a sale or conveyance of the property. The FNMA/FHLMC Deed of Trust also prohibits a long term lease or a lease with an option to buy.

EASEMENT - The right to use the land of another for a specific limited purpose. Examples include utility lines, driveways, and INGRESS AND EGRESS. Easements can be temporary or permanent.

EMINENT DOMAIN - The power of the state to take private property for public use upon payment of just compensation.

ENCROACHMENT - The physical intrusion of a structure or improvement on the land of another. Examples include a fence or driveway over the property line.

ENCUMBRANCE - Any lien, liability or charge against a property.

EQUITY SHARING - A form of joint ownership between an owner/occupant and an owner/investor. The investor takes depreciation deductions for his share of the ownership. The occupant receives a portion of the tax write-offs for interest and taxes and a part of his monthly payment is treated as rent. The co-owners divide the profit upon sale of the property. Compare, JOINT OWNERSHIP.

ESCHEAT - Property that reverts to the state when an individual dies with heirs and without a will.

ESCROW - A disinterested third party holds funds or documents on behalf of others and subject to their instructions.

EXECUTOR - A person named in a will to carry out its terms and administer the estate. Depending upon the terms of the Will, the Executor may not have power to sell the real estate; that power may rest in the individual heirs. The feminine form is Executrix. Compare, ADMINISTRATOR.

FEDERAL HOME LOAN MORTGAGE CORPORATION - A affiliate of the Federal Home loan Bank which purchases FHA and VA loans from members of the Federal Reserve System and the Federal Home Loan Bank Systems.

FEE SIMPLE - The absolute total interest in real property. Compare, LIFE ESTATE, REVERSION.

FINANCING STATEMENT - Lenders record financing statements to evidence personal property is subject to a lien. The company who finances a new furnace, siding or windows may record the financing statement to evidence they have not been fully paid for.

FIXTURES - An item of personal property attached to real property so that it can not be removed without damage to the real property. It then becomes a part of the real property.

FORECLOSURE - The process by which a lender sells property securing a loan in order to repay the loan. Under a DEED OF TRUST, foreclosure is by public auction after appropriate advertisement. A MORTGAGE may require the lender obtain Court approval prior to sale.

FULLY INDEXED NOTE RATE - The index value of an adjustable rate loan plus the gross margin stated in the note.

GENERAL WARRANTY DEED - The Grantor warrants title against all claims. In Virginia, this warranty includes claims all the way back in time to the King of England. Compare, QUIT CLAIM DEED, SPECIAL WARRANTY DEED.

GRADUATE PAYMENT MORTGAGE

Provides for partially deferred payments of principal or lower interest rates at the start of a loan. These are not considered ADJUSTABLE RATE LOANS because the rates are fixed and known.

GROUND LEASE - The owner grants a long term lease of the land (usually 99 years) and allows the lessee to build and use the land as agreed. At the end of the term, the land and all improvements revert to the owner.

GUARDIAN - One appointed by the Court to administer the affairs of a minor. A guardian ad litem is appointed to protect one's interest in a particular legal action. See, CONSERVATOR.

HIATUS - A gap or space left between two parcels of land and not included in the legal description of either parcel. Similar terms are Gaps and Gores.

HOMESTEAD DEED - A declaration filed in the land records that an individual is asserting his homestead exemption. That exemption allows one to protect up to $5,000 in assets (plus $500 per dependent) against the claims of creditors.

INITIAL NOTE RATE -The note rate upon origination of an adjustable rate loan. This rate is sometimes called a "teaser rate" and is usually less than the fully indexed rate.

INGRESS AND EGRESS - Applied to EASEMENTS, meaning the right to go in and out over a piece of property but not the right to park on it.

INSURABLE TITLE - Title subject to a defect or claim which a title insurance company is willing to insure against. Compare, MARKETABLE TITLE.

INSURED CLOSING LETTER - An indemnity given to a lender from a title insurance company, agreeing to be responsible if the closing agent does not follow the lender's instructions or misappropriates the loan proceeds. Lender's usually require an insured closing letter be on file for each settlement.

INTESTATE - An estate without a Will. Compare, TESTATE

JOINT OWNERSHIP AGREEMENT - An agreement between owners defining their rights and responsibilities. The agreement could be between an investor and an occupant or among occupants. If an investor is involved, the investor does not take depreciation deductions and none of the occupant's payment is deemed rent for tax purposes. Compare, EQUITY SHARING. We always recommend a written joint ownership agreement when unmarried parties acquire property.

JOINT TENANCY - Two or more persons own a property. Joint tenants with the common law right of survivorship means the survivor inherits the property without reference to the decedent's will. Creditors may sue to have the property divided to settle claims against one of the owners. Compare, TENANTS IN COMMON, TENANTS BY THE ENTIRETY.

JUDGMENT LIEN - A judgment automatically becomes a lien against all real property owned by the judgment debtor in the county where the judgment is docketed (recorded). The STATUTE OF LIMITATIONS for a judgment (in Virginia) is ten years after conveyance of a property or twenty years after entry of the judgment whichever first occurs.

LAND CONTRACT - See, CONTRACT FOR DEED.

LENDER'S TITLE INSURANCE - A TITLE INSURANCE policy covering the lender for the loan amount. The coverage declines as the loan is paid down and when the loan is paid off, there is no further coverage.

LIEN - A claim or charge against property. Property is said to be encumbered by a lien and the lien must be removed to clear title.

LIFE CAP - A ceiling the note rate of an adjustable rate loan.

LIFE ESTATE - The right to use, occupy and own for the life of an individual. Compare, FEE SIMPLE.

MAJORITY - The age at which a person is entitled to handle his own affairs. In Virginia, the age is 18. If a minor holds title to property, the Court will have to appoint a Guardian to determine if sale or financing is in the best interest of the minor.

MARKETABLE TITLE - Title without defects or claims so as to be readily accepted without fair or reasonable doubt. Compare, INSURABLE TITLE.

MECHANIC'S LIENS - The right of an unpaid contractor, laborer or supplier to file a lien against property to recover the value of his work. Virginia allows the claimant to file the lien after title has passed to the new owner and gives the lien priority over the new owner's interest.

METES AND BOUNDS - A means of describing land by directions and distances rather than reference to a lot number. Generally used when land has not been subdivided into lots.

MORTGAGE - A voluntary lien filed against property to secure a debt, usually a loan. To foreclose, the lender must often institute a court action and the borrower may have the right to reclaim the property after foreclosure. Lenders in Virginia use DEEDS OF TRUST rather than mortgages. Compare, DEED OF TRUST.

NEGATIVE AMORTIZATION - When the monthly installments are insufficient to pay the interest, so that the unpaid interest must be added to the principal.

NOTE - A written promise to pay a certain sum of money at a certain time. A negotiable note starts "Pay to the order of" and is transferable by endorsement similar to a check.

NOTARY PUBLIC - One authorized by law to acknowledge and certify documents and signatures. Virginia does not require an applicant pass a test to become a notary.

OWNER'S TITLE INSURANCE - A policy of TITLE INSURANCE for the buyer insuring the full purchase price of the property. The owner's policy usually contains an inflation endorsement automatically increasing the coverage each year to keep up with inflation, up to a maximum of 150% of the original policy amount. The insurance premium is paid at settlement, and the coverage continues forever.

PARTITION - The forced division of land among parties who were formerly co-owners. A partition suit may ask to divide the land or if that is not practical, sell the land and divide the proceeds.

PLAT - A map showing the division of a piece of land with lots, streets and, if applicable, common area.

PIPESTEM LOT - A lot connected to a public street by a narrow strip of land. Usually several adjacent pipestems are combined to form one driveway with each owner having a mutual-reciprocal easement to use and maintain the driveway to the street.

POWER OF ATTORNEY - A written document authorizing another to act on his behalf as an ATTORNEY IN FACT. One does not need to be a licensed attorney to act as an attorney in fact but, power of attorney forms are legal documents and should only be prepared by a licensed attorney.

PREPAYMENT PENALTY - An additional charge imposed by the lender for paying off a loan before the due date.

PRIVATE MORTGAGE INSURANCE - Mortgage guaranty insurance to protect the lender against default. This usually is required on loans where the loan amount exceeds 80% of the value of the property.

QUIET TITLE ACTION - A suit brought to remove a claim or objection on title.

QUITCLAIM DEED - A deed releasing whatever interest you may hold in a property but making no warranty whatsoever. Compare, SPECIAL WARRANTY DEED and GENERAL WARRANTY DEED.

RE-ISSUE RATE - A discounted rate for title insurance when the title was previously insured with an owner's title insurance policy issued within the last ten years.

REMAINDER - An interest in land that is postponed until the termination of some other interest such as a LIFE ESTATE. Compare, FEE SIMPLE.

REVERSION - A provision in a conveyance that the land will return to the grantor, or his heirs, upon the happening of an event or contingency. Compare, FEE SIMPLE.

RIPARIAN RIGHTS - The rights of an owner of land adjacent to water.

SPECIAL WARRANTY DEED - The seller warrants he has done nothing to impair title but makes no warranty before his ownership. Builders, trustees and estates often grant by special warranty deed. This is not a concern so long as the buyer gets an OWNER'S TITLE INSURANCE POLICY. Compare, GENERAL WARRANTY DEED AND QUITCLAIM DEED.

STATUTE OF LIMITATIONS - The time period to file a law suit to enforce a claim or it is barred by law.

SUBDIVISION - Dividing land into lots and streets. The owner signs a PLAT and Deed of Resubdivision which is recorded among the land records. The state and county have strict requirements for subdivision of land.

SUBJECT TO - Taking title to property with a lien but not agreeing to be personally responsible for the lien. If the holder who forecloses the lien can take the property but may not collect any money from the owner who took "subject to." Compare, ASSUMPTION.

SURVEY – the drawing of the house on the lot. Actually, there are many different types of surveys. The one most often used is a "house location" or "physical improvements" survey. To contrast, "boundary" surveys only locate the property lines not the improvements.

TENANTS BY THE ENTIRETY - A husband and wife own the property with the common law right of survivorship so, if one dies, the other automatically inherits. One may not sue the other to PARTITION the property. A creditor of one may not claim the property or the proceeds of sale. Compare, TENANT IN COMMON, JOINT TENANTS.

TENANT IN COMMON - Two or more persons own the property with no right of survivorship. If one dies, his interest passes to his heirs, not necessarily the co-owner. Either party, or a creditor of one, may sue to PARTITION the property. Compare, TENANTS BY THE ENTIRETY, JOINT TENANTS.

TESTATE - To die with a Will. Compare, INTESTATE.

TESTATOR - One who makes out a last will and testament. The feminine form is Testatrix.

TITLE INSURANCE - Insurance against loss or damage as a result of defect in title ownership to a particular piece of property. Title insurance covers mistakes made during a TITLE SEARCH as well as matters which could not be found or discovered in the public records such as missing heirs, mistakes, fraud and forgery.

TITLE SEARCH - An examination of the public records, including court decisions, to disclose facts concerning the ownership of real estate. The title examiner prepares an ABSTRACT and the title agent prepares a BINDER but decisions regarding the legal sufficiency of title or questions requiring legal interpretation must be resolved by a licensed attorney at law.

TRUST - A right to or in property held for the benefit of another. A trust may be written or implied. An implied trust is called a Constructive Trust.

TRUSTEE - One who holds property in Trust for another. In Virginia, you may hold title to real property as TRUSTEE without revealing the BENEFICIARY'S identity and provided, the Deed you receive grants you full trust powers to deal with the property, no one will question your authority.

USURY - Charging more than the maximum legally permitted rate of interest. There is no usury limit for loans secured by a first trust.

WRAPAROUND - The debt secured includes an existing debt already on the property. The payments made to the holder of the wraparound include payments due on the existing loan and the holder must forward the appropriate portion of each payment to the existing noteholder. Often used to avoid a PREPAYMENT PENALTY or a DUE ON SALE CLAUSE. Can be used to refer to a wraparound DEED OF TRUST or CONTRACT FOR DEED.

ZONING - Regulation of private land use and development by local government.

THIRTY YEAR FACTOR TABLE

To find the monthly payment, divide the loan amount
by 1,000 and multiply the result by the factor below.

RATE	FACTOR	RATE	FACTOR	RATE	FACTOR
======	======	======	======	======	======
4.000%	$4.77	8.000%	$7.34	12.000%	$10.29
4.125%	$4.85	8.125%	$7.42	12.125%	$10.38
4.250%	$4.92	8.250%	$7.51	12.250%	$10.48
4.375%	$4.99	8.375%	$7.60	12.375%	$10.58
4.500%	$5.07	8.500%	$7.69	12.500%	$10.67
4.625%	$5.14	8.625%	$7.78	12.625%	$10.77
4.750%	$5.22	8.750%	$7.87	12.750%	$10.87
4.875%	$5.29	8.875%	$7.96	12.875%	$10.96
5.000%	$5.37	9.000%	$8.05	13.000%	$11.06
5.125%	$5.44	9.125%	$8.14	13.125%	$11.16
5.250%	$5.52	9.250%	$8.23	13.250%	$11.26
5.375%	$5.60	9.375%	$8.32	13.375%	$11.36
5.500%	$5.68	9.500%	$8.41	13.500%	$11.45
5.625%	$5.76	9.625%	$8.50	13.625%	$11.55
5.750%	$5.84	9.750%	$8.59	13.750%	$11.65
5.875%	$5.92	9.875%	$8.68	13.875%	$11.75
6.000%	$6.00	10.000%	$8.78	14.000%	$11.85
6.125%	$6.08	10.125%	$8.87	14.125%	$11.95
6.250%	$6.16	10.250%	$8.96	14.250%	$12.05
6.375%	$6.24	10.375%	$9.05	14.375%	$12.15
6.500%	$6.32	10.500%	$9.15	14.500%	$12.25
6.625%	$6.40	10.625%	$9.24	14.625%	$12.35
6.750%	$6.49	10.750%	$9.33	14.750%	$12.44
6.875%	$6.57	10.875%	$9.43	14.875%	$12.54
7.000%	$6.65	11.000%	$9.52	15.000%	$12.64
7.125%	$6.74	11.125%	$9.62	15.125%	$12.74
7.250%	$6.82	11.250%	$9.71	15.250%	$12.84
7.375%	$6.91	11.375%	$9.81	15.375%	$12.94
7.500%	$6.99	11.500%	$9.90	15.500%	$13.05
7.625%	$7.08	11.625%	$10.00	15.625%	$13.15
7.750%	$7.16	11.750%	$10.09	15.750%	$13.25
7.875%	$7.25	11.875%	$10.19	15.875%	$13.35
8.000%	$7.34	12.000%	$10.29	16.000%	$13.45

FIFTEEN YEAR FACTOR TABLE

To find the monthly payment, divide the loan amount
by 1,000 and multiply the result by the factor below.

RATE	FACTOR	RATE	FACTOR	RATE	FACTOR
======	======	======	======	======	======
4.000%	$7.40	8.000%	$9.56	12.000%	$12.00
4.125%	$7.46	8.125%	$9.63	12.125%	$12.08
4.250%	$7.52	8.250%	$9.70	12.250%	$12.16
4.375%	$7.59	8.375%	$9.77	12.375%	$12.24
4.500%	$7.65	8.500%	$9.85	12.500%	$12.33
4.625%	$7.71	8.625%	$9.92	12.625%	$12.41
4.750%	$7.78	8.750%	$9.99	12.750%	$12.49
4.875%	$7.84	8.875%	$10.07	12.875%	$12.57
5.000%	$7.91	9.000%	$10.14	13.000%	$12.65
5.125%	$7.97	9.125%	$10.22	13.125%	$12.73
5.250%	$8.04	9.250%	$10.29	13.250%	$12.82
5.375%	$8.10	9.375%	$10.37	13.375%	$12.90
5.500%	$8.17	9.500%	$10.44	13.500%	$12.98
5.625%	$8.24	9.625%	$10.52	13.625%	$13.07
5.750%	$8.30	9.750%	$10.59	13.750%	$13.15
5.875%	$8.37	9.875%	$10.67	13.875%	$13.23
6.000%	$8.44	10.000%	$10.75	14.000%	$13.32
6.125%	$8.51	10.125%	$10.82	14.125%	$13.40
6.250%	$8.57	10.250%	$10.90	14.250%	$13.49
6.375%	$8.64	10.375%	$10.98	14.375%	$13.57
6.500%	$8.71	10.500%	$11.05	14.500%	$13.66
6.625%	$8.78	10.625%	$11.13	14.625%	$13.74
6.750%	$8.85	10.750%	$11.21	14.750%	$13.83
6.875%	$8.92	10.875%	$11.29	14.875%	$13.91
7.000%	$8.99	11.000%	$11.37	15.000%	$14.00
7.125%	$9.06	11.125%	$11.44	15.125%	$14.08
7.250%	$9.13	11.250%	$11.52	15.250%	$14.17
7.375%	$9.20	11.375%	$11.60	15.375%	$14.25
7.500%	$9.27	11.500%	$11.68	15.500%	$14.34
7.625%	$9.34	11.625%	$11.76	15.625%	$14.43
7.750%	$9.41	11.750%	$11.84	15.750%	$14.51
7.875%	$9.48	11.875%	$11.92	15.875%	$14.60
8.000%	$9.56	12.000%	$12.00	16.000%	$14.69

TO ORDER THE MOST RECENT EDITION OF THE REAL ESTATE CONTRACTS HANDBOOK, PLEASE VISIT AMAZON.COM

CPSIA information can be obtained at www.ICGtesting.com
Printed in the USA
LVOW131936100112

263224LV00007BA/27/P